PILOT-DIPLOMAT
AND
GARAGE RAT

The author in 1939

PILOT-DIPLOMAT
AND
GARAGE RAT

Air Commodore
H. M. (Toby) Pearson, CBE

MERLIN BOOKS LTD.
Braunton   Devon

*To my dear wife ELIZABETH
for the many tasks she undertook
in the preparation of this book.
Without her tolerance and understanding,
it would never have been completed.*

ISBN 0 86303 445-4
Printed in England by Antony Rowe Ltd., Chippenham, Wilts.

FOREWORD
by Marshal of the Royal Air Force Sir Dermot Boyle, GCB, KCVO, KBE, AFC

This book covers the life of the author from his early days in the Argentine, through his time in the RAF, from his entry to the RAF (Cadet) College until his retirement in 1955.

The author was in Fighter Command during the critical time of the Battle of Britain and later in night air defence. He gives a very good account of the working of radar and electronic countermeasures at a time when he was involved in that aspect of the Command's work.

The author's upbringing in the Argentine, which gave him knowledge of Spanish, had interesting and exciting repercussions during his career: first in Peru where he went in 1934 to help set up the Peruvian Air Force Cadet School, later he became involved in the Spanish Civil War, and then after the Second World War was the British Air Attaché in Peru.

A very interesting and informative book.

Dermot Boyle

CONTENTS

ILLUSTRATIONS

INTRODUCTION
by Air Commodore J. A. Leathart CB, DSO

There are certain people in life who, by design or destiny, are always near at hand to share one's experiences and exercise a lasting influence on one's views and deeds.

I first met Toby Pearson when he was posted to command No. 54 Squadron based at Hornchurch in March 1938. I had been with the squadron since November 1937 so we were comparatively new boys together, and had a lot to learn. I took over command to 54 Squadron when Toby was promoted and posted to HQ No. 11 Group.

We were both married in May 1939 and were together at HQ Fighter Command at Bentley Priory. We both had command of Beaufighter night fighter squadrons and were members of 85 Group Headquarters during the invasion. We served also in France, Belgium and Holland.

In 1970 I retired from the RAF and joined Toby in a business venture, which was not very successful, but I bought a house near his, and we still see each other now and again.

His book has an odd title, but I think this is explained adequately in the early chapters. It is different from most war books in that it records periods of his life while still in the RAF, but serving as advisor or air attaché in foreign lands where Spanish is spoken. There are also several events which show the humorous side to his story, which makes pleasant and easy reading.

ACKNOWLEDGEMENTS

I wish to acknowledge the help and advice given to me in the preparation of this book, by the following persons:
Marshal of the Royal Air Force Sir Dermot Boyle GCB, KCVO, KBE, AFC
Group Captain John Cunningham CBE, DSO, DFC and Bar
Air Commodore Rory Chisholm CBE, DSO, DFC and Bar
Air Commodore J. A. Leathart CB, DSO
The late Air Commodore F. V. West VC, CBE, MC
Lord Kings Norton
Group Captain M. V. Clube
Major P. R. Reid MBE, MC
My thanks are due also to my son James and my stepson Anthony Griffiths for their continuing encouragement and support.
Mrs P. Dawe for typing and retyping the drafts.
My niece, Maxine Woodgate, for copies of photographs of my two brothers.
Aeroplane Monthly for permission to reprint photographs first published in their 'Personal Album' in February 1986.
Motor Sport for permission to reprint photographs first published of the 'Austin Whippet' in September 1980.
Iain Hutton-Jamieson for the book jacket design

CHAPTER I

It was my stepson Anthony who persuaded me to write down some of my exploits and reminiscences. My own three children had heard them all before and were inclined to say, the moment I opened my mouth, "What, Dad, not number 22 again!" but not so Anthony, who seemed to be an interested and attentive listener and I therefore agreed to try to write a book. Not an autobiography, too many people have done that, but a chronological account of amusing circumstances and important incidents that have happened to me, with a degree of embellishment. So here goes —

In the beginning:

In 1895 or thereabouts, my father went from Australia to the Argentine with a bag of gold coins. These belonged to an aunt of his who lived in Dorset, UK, and was interested in acquiring land there for breeding cattle. At that time the Argentine government gave land away to anyone who would provide the infrastructure necessary for an *estancia*: that meant fencing, water supply, water storage, accommodation and various other essential items of equipment. Since all the railways were British owned and British managed it was not difficult to assess the chances of the railway coming through the land to be acquired. Railways were necessary for transporting the cattle to the processing factories prior to shipment as carcasses to the UK and any schoolboy atlas will show the extent of the network of railways leading out from Buenos Aires to the pampas.

For eighteen years my father managed and developed the land acquired and then it was sold, so no doubt his aunt in Dorset made a good profit. In 1912 he went to manage another bigger *estancia*, which belonged to relatives of my mother. I was four years old at the time and my elder brother Alec was six. The *estancia* was called 'Santa Inez' and it is from here that I begin to remember.

We lived in the large house with a tennis court, swimming pool and polo ground. In 1916 my brother and I were sent to school at St George's College, Quilmes, ten miles out from Buenos Aires. The Headmaster, Canon Stevenson known as 'The Gun', was an impressive personality, but because of the 1914-18 war in Europe he did not have the support of a loyal and qualified staff. Also he was obliged to take boys from the age of seven to eighteen, as there was no preparatory school. The head boy, when we went there was Alfred Mulcahy. He was over six feet tall and highly respected by both boys and staff, and I was the youngest boy, just seven years old. Little did I know that Alfred was to become my brother-in-law.

The most revered building in the school was the Chapel, and to 'The Gun' a church service was the most important event of the day. He had a Victorian outlook on religion and woe betide any boy who misbehaved during his services. Nevertheless the bigger boys would sometime take advantage of the smaller ones to exercise their pranks, even in Chapel. I remember one Sunday morning we were sent to collect bumble-bees in the gardens and put them into test tubes taken from the science lab. In Chapel the big boys were at the back, then came the small boys, and then in the front two rows were the girls from Cricklewood, the English school near by. The Chapel was dark with a large window above the altar, where the sun came in. During the service and particularly while the Creed was being recited, bumble-bees were released from the test tubes one by one. They would fly immediately towards the light, which meant narrowly missing the heads of the various members of the congregation pass over the heads of the small boys, and girls and then up over the choir. Everybody ducked and they reached the window and hit it with a resounding thud, very like the doodle-bugs in the Second World War.

On another occasion, the big boys instructed us smaller ones to take the shoes off certain selected girls during prayers. This was easy to do because we sat immediately behind them and when they were kneeling down the shoes came off silently; only one shoe would be taken. I might get an instruction to remove the shoe from Betty or some other girl who was well known, because many of the boys had sisters and cousins at Cricklewood. The shoe would then be passed back to the big boy who had demanded it and when the service ended the poor girl had to hobble out of Chapel to join the crocodile for the march back to Cricklewood. The big boy would toss her shoe back to her at the exit gate.

Because of the distance some boys had to travel, there were only two terms a year, one of four months and one of four and a half months. I was homesick and these terms were very long for a small boy but in 1922 our family, which by then numbered five children, came home and settled down in Sussex.

I should at this stage dwell on our family circumstances when we came back from the Argentine to Sussex. Although we were not poor, my father had diabetes and at that time insulin was very expensive and there was no NHS. He needed two injections every week. My elder brother was at Brighton College and I at Cheltenham College, and school fees had to be paid. There were three younger ones, particularly my sister Clare, who was born in 1910 to be considered. On the other hand, we had several relatives including my father's two sisters in Scotland, his aunt already mentioned and others, who were reasonably well off. As for myself, I found that I spent holidays either at home with my family or with my father's relations, the one comfortable but not given to luxury, and the other much better off. She was very interested in us children from the Argentine and able to contribute to our education and advancement, and have us to stay.

During my time in the RAF I always benefited from being able to speak Spanish which has led to several interesting appointments. At St George's, the language was mainly English, but there were boys who could not speak English at all and there were others who spoke both English and Spanish at home. We spoke English at Santa Inez where our English nanny looked after us. There were probably not more than thirty employees which included the peons (jacks of all trades) and the gauchos who drove and rounded up the cattle; some of them lived in small remote cottages spread throughout the *estancia*.

I had not studied Spanish at that time, but picked up the 'kitchen' version, with an Argentine accent, which gave me a basis to understand and pronounce the language. Later I took some Spanish lessons and learned to write as well as speak it. Of course those who lived in Buenos Aires or any large town, had much more opportunity to speak Spanish fluently. The gauchos and peons spoke a very primitive version of the language and although it was colourful every other word was what we in Britain would call a four letter one!

At Cheltenham College I profited from the environment and from the boys I met and in a way, it was an introduction to my new life in Britain. I was above the average age for entry to a public school but those things were overlooked directly after the First World War. I was happy there and managed to pass essential exams. The college at that time, was dedicated to the Army, and boasted more scholarships and passes than any other public school into the Royal Military Acadamy Woolwich. Whether it was true or not I don't know, but Cheltenham town was a favourite habitat for retired Army officers. It was a bit of a shock to my housemaster therefore,

14

to hear that I intended to go into the Royal Air Force.

The only activity at which I excelled was boxing and although I won a few cups I disliked the sport and I never kept it up since. My younger brother Max, was at the Junior School so I took him out for walks on Sundays. We had splendid facilities in Charlton Park and Leckhampton. In 1925 my father died from pneumonia and this was a bigger blow to Max than to me, because Max had lived at Santa Inez while I was at St George's and he had accompanied my father on his rounds in the Model T Fords that we had there. He was very close to my father and took his death badly but came to terms with it.

In examinations for entering the armed forces, the Army exam qualified for Cranwell as well, and although my family, and my aunts in Scotland particularly, wanted me to join the Army I did not relish the thought of soldiering for the rest of my life. I fancied flying and also it seemed to me that the RAF had much more comfortable clothes than those we wore in the OTC! Such simple things are an influence at the age of 16, my elder brother was already in the RAF on a short service commission and had the flying bug which I got later. He went into civil flying which I never managed to do.

CHAPTER II

Cranwell 1926-27

Although closely associated with flying, only 70-80 hours spread over two years was done by each cadet at Cranwell. At the flying training schools of which there were four, the same number of hours were flown by each pupil in one year. It was made known to us cadets that flying aeroplanes was not the be-all and end-all of our presence there, so we were expected to acquire a working knowledge of the sciences, the Arts, history, etc. We were also encouraged to take part in the many sports for which excellent facilities were provided. Indeed our teams had an enviable record of successes in our matches particularly when we beat both the 'Shop' and the Royal Military College, Sandhurst at rugger, the most prestigious game of all.

The average cadet, and I include myself, could not compete with Frank Whittle in Science and Mathematics, nor with Douglas Bader in the field of sport. These are just two who lived to become famous, but there were several others who, had they survived, could have contributed to mankind. I name Reggie Elsmie, Pussy Shelley, Red Scarlett and Guy Charles in this category. Also, a contemporary and close friend, was Teddy Hudleston whose meteoric career from Pilot Officer to Air Chief Marshal should go into the Guinness Book of Records. He was a true scholar/athlete and he did survive. But these were the top names in learning and in sport, whereas I was an average cadet and did not wear the colourful blazer which identified the sportsman who excelled, or go into the class-room carrying a learned thesis under my arm which identified a scholar. So I became instead 'The Garage Rat'.

Every cadet was encouraged, in fact expected to have a motor bicycle, and motor cars were not permitted. If you did not have a motor bike of your own, you would be issued with one from the pool which was kept for cadets in a hangar. These were P & Ms having been used by dispatch riders during the 1914-18 war of which there must have been a large surplus. They were not very reliable, although legend claims that one cadet rode his to London and back during a weekend. The most the average cadet could do with his P & M was about twelve miles, after which it became hotter and hotter and he would have to stop riding for half an hour to let it cool down. I was fortunate and had my own motor bike but in my last term I decided that I would prefer a motor car which was not allowed.

So I said to myself, why not buy a motor bicycle and sidecar and convert it so that you drove the combination from the sidecar where you could wrap up nice and warm, and not be exposed to the elements? I bought an old AJS twin cylinder and a sidecar which didn't cost very much, but there was the big task ahead in doing the conversion. Fortunately I had the use of the cadets' workshop where we were instructed in practical engineering. This was kept open for any engineering project that any cadet had in mind. I made full use of this facility and by means of lots of 'Emmet' and 'Heath Robinson' equipment, spindles, bowden cables, rods, etc., I managed to get the full control of the combination into the sidecar, steering wheel, throttle, brakes and gears — and it worked. The difficulty was that the gear box was faulty. This had nothing to do with my conversion, but I didn't have enough money to get a new gearbox; in fact the machine was so old that I doubt whether one existed. I did manage to drive, from the sidecar, down local roads and I went to Digby once where my elder brother was an officer, which is about ten or fifteen miles away. I called the combination Boanerges, which attracted a great deal of attention, especially on local roads, where one seldom met motor cars in those days. However, when someone saw this combination, without a driver on the motor bike, it made him wonder how much alcohol he had consumed that day!

CHAPTER III

Calshot 1929

I was commissioned from the RAF College, Cranwell at the end of 1928 and with five other ex-Flight Cadets posted to the flying boat course at RAF Calshot for which all six of us had applied. It was the year of the Schneider Trophy and Calshot was the place to be, but also our course on flying boats and navigation was of abundant interest; alighting for lunch at Plymouth one day, the Scillies another, Guernsey another and now and then longer two-day trips to the Firth of Forth via Felixstowe.

Those days, with no war on the horizon, may in retrospect have been irresponsible. But what else for us youths to do but improve our knowledge and our friendships? There were many friends from Cranwell who took part in the flying which went on inland in the UK and overseas.

One of these was 'Girly' Leach in a fighter squadron based at Tangmere. He was a year senior to me at Cranwell and flew his small aeroplane from Hamble, across Southampton Water from Calshot. On his recommendation I became a member of the Hamble Flying Club. 'Girly's' aeroplane was an Avro Baby, one of six built for the 1923 competition at Lympne, powered by a 4-cylinder ADC engine (Cirrus) and had one cockpit with two seats in tandem, the passenger sat as if riding pillion on a motor cycle clinging to the belly of the pilot. His favourite pastime was to approach Hamble from under the trees and bob up over the airfield, but he stopped this when someone explained to him that there was a road under the trees along which a double-decker bus passed every fifteen minutes. Sad to relate my good friend died in hospital from a kidney ailment towards the end of the year. It was at Hamble that I qualified for my civil pilot's licence No. 1879 dated 25th May 1929, which I still hold, but doubt whether it is still valid!

And so to the Austin Whippet. Although I had no money beyond my Pilot Officer's pay of £34 a month, I was determined to buy a light aeroplane of my own. First I explored the rejects from the 1923 Lympne competition, without success. Then someone told me that an Austin Whippet was for sale at Castle Bromwich. I had not heard of this make of aeroplane before, but off I went one weekend to Birmingham.

It was just what I wanted, folding wings, single seater and tubular steel frame. It looked a bit grubby, but I was sure I could put that right once I got it to Calshot. I did not meet the owner and dealt with a Flying Club representative. We agreed a price of £50 to be paid at £5 per month for ten months. He explained to me that the previous engine was a 45 h.p. Anzani but it was underpowered and a 50 or 60 h.p. Anzani engine had been installed. Both these engines had suction inlet valves and the oil sprayed over the fuselage. He gave me the pump from the previous 45 h.p. engine and suggested that it might reduce the excessive oil flow. I flew round one circuit, landed and then took off and headed south. I found that 70 m.p.h. was the best cruising speed.

My first stop was Upper Heyford near Oxford and the second Worthydown near Winchester. I had telephoned friends at both these RAF stations in advance so, being a weekend, they arranged for fuel to be available. From Worthydown, I set course for Calshot. There was a small field just behind the Officers' Mess and the farmer had agreed that I may land there once and that is what I did. I had alerted 'Red' Scarlett who owned an Austin Seven sports car and was one of my Cranwell contemporaries. His father was a very senior RAF (Ex-RNAS) officer still serving at that time.

'Red' met me on the field and we found no difficulty in fixing the tail skid of the Austin Whippet into the boot of the Austin Seven, and we towed the aircraft to the car-park of the Officers' Mess, where it stayed until the following weekend. During the week, and whenever I had any spare time, I looked for more permanent accommodation where I could work on my new acquisition and rejuvenate it.

I found an empty shed, an annexe to one of the flying boat hangars, and the following weekend 'Red' and I towed the Whippet down the spit to its new quarters. One morning, during the following week, I was summoned to the presence of the Flight Commander and received a mild rebuke for planting my aircraft on property under his jurisdiction, without his permission or indeed any permission whatsoever. However, Bill Staton agreed, after my apology, that I may continue to enjoy the temporary occupation of these desirable premises. I now had to concentrate on the task of rejuvenation.

My first impulse was to have the old and oil-stained fabric replaced. There was a fabric section at Calshot, where they could have made a highly professional job on the wings and fuselage, but the officer in charge, although sympathetic, needed approval from higher authority, and that was not forthcoming. Next I needed a new length of 'bungie' for the undercarriage suspension. I found in the stores a stock of this, which although unused and unsoiled, had been condemned and classified as scrap. I helped myself to what I needed. In short I cleaned and painted where I could, took bits apart and put them together again as best I could, and washed the fabric where I could. What is more I changed the oil pump to the one given to me at Castle Bromwich which came off the 45 h.p. engine. I had in fact returned to being a 'Garage Rat'.

While I was doing all this in the evenings and during the weekends, life was hotting up at Calshot with the advent of the High Speed Flight, commanded by Squadron Leader Orlebar. It seems to me, in retrospect, that the selection of the six officers destined to win the Schneider Trophy outright, was made not only on account of their brilliant airmanship, but also their personality and humour. No doubt the few NCOs and airmen in the flight were selected on these merits also, but most of the maintenance was done by engineers from the manufacturers of the airframes, engines and components. Nevertheless, these and their Italian counterparts appeared to enjoy the atmosphere which prevailed at Calshot at that time. The Italians from Macchi on Lake Varese were slightly bewildered at first, but made close friends at Calshot which continued even after the war.

We, the Pilot Officers on the flying boat course, were three or four years junior to those in the High Speed Flight. We admired their skill and we giggled at their pranks but took no active part in them. I will record a few anecdotes.

First the High Speed Pole — the aquatic sports at Calshot were a serious annual event and one of the races was the pole race. Each Flight detailed eight stalwart men to propel one telegraph pole and having lined up the swimmers with their poles on the slipway, under starter's orders, the race began. The object was to push or paddle the pole round a buoy about 100 yards out and back to the slipway. Of course the High Speed Flight had their own High Speed Pole! which had been kept under a tarpaulin, just where the sentry paced up and down in front of the High Speed hangar. None of us knew what was under the tarpaulin until the big day came. All the other competitors were there with naked poles but the High Speed Flight with their pole still under the tarpaulin. The starter shouted "ready, steady," and fired his pistol. Then the High Speed Flight discarded secrecy and revealed all. A bracket held a small propeller and further back was a second bracket to which a length of bungie was secured; probably the bungie came from the same stock where I had acquired mine for my Austin Whippet.

The propeller seemed to be well primed, the bungie knotted into contortions like so many sparrows' kneecaps. We could all be certain that the High Speed Pole would take a bold leap forward on entering the water, and with the acknowledged physique of the crew, would win the race. Sad to relate whoever wound the propeller did so anti-clockwise instead of clockwise and on entering the water the High Speed Pole shot backwards on to the slipway. They finished last in the race, if at all.

Next, there was the .22 pistol. Its charge was a blank cartridge, its bullet was a masticated chewing gum pellet and its target was the bottom of someone senior, pompous and fat. Having decided on the victim, the object was to persuade him to bend over and then 'ping'. There were plenty of potential targets about, but one of the planning principles was that nobody should know 'who done it'. So, one day, a victim arrived in the Flight Commander's office and a half-crown was there on the floor in front of the desk. The pilots were studying a chart of Southampton Water, the CO was at his desk, the victim bent down to pick up the half-crown saying, "Someone has been throwing his money about." 'Ping' went the pistol, "Ouch!" went the victim, "Lovely weather we are having!" said the pilots, now looking with even more interest at the chart of Southampton Water than ever before.

There was to be a guest night and sing-song around the piano in the Officers' Mess. The music was selected from popular songs of the day. The score was there for the pianist to play. The lyric was in very small print. The victim, who was enjoying his part in the singing, bent down lower and lower to read the words. He presented a fabulous target and then 'ping'. The carpet on which he had been standing was pulled away so he rolled over still rubbing his sore behind. Naturally the High Speed Flight was full of compassion for the victim and offered him another drink.

During my evenings and weekends at work on my Austin Whippet, I was visited several times by Dick Atcherley (Batchy), who was always interested in light aeroplanes and a prominent member of the High Speed Flight. He offered to take me into Southampton in his car — the very car his colleagues had given him as a birthday joke. It was a Bean, but he called it the 'Has Been', so off we went. About half-way to Southampton the car refused to turn right although to turn left presented no problem. There was no future in continuing, so we got out to diagnose the problem and it was soon apparent that the front axle had become detached from its suspension spring. Dick thereupon gave the offside wheel several sharp kicks, to even things up, and dived into his tool chest, from which he produced a large coil of copper wire. He wired the axle to the suspension and off we went. It seems that, in his fertile mind, a coil of copper wire was the solution to many engineering problems. He told me on the way back that he intended to enter the 'Has Been' for the London-Exeter rally, copper wire and all, but whether he ever did, I do not know.

At last my Austin Whippet, now painted light green and silver, was ready to fly again, but from where? The spit which connected Calshot Castle, with its hangar workshops and slipways, to the living accommodation, was over a mile long but was only wide enough to take the road and miniature railway. On one side was the sea and on the other mud flats.

I noticed a small patch of grass on the mud flats where a farmer had, at some time, tried to reclaim the land. It was near the road and had a hard dry surface, which would allow 75 yards for take off. Dick and Red were there to help and we towed and then manhandled the aeroplane to its point of departure. We waved goodbye and it was airborne with yards to spare. Ten minutes later I landed at Hamble.

Here, several problems arose. There was to be a fee for hangarage and I would not be allowed to use Hamble as a base until the Certificate of Airworthiness was renewed. The Club Flying Instructor, Captain Swaffer, said he would like to test my aeroplane, to which I readily agreed. When taxiing out for take off, the undercarriage collapsed so it seems that the bungie which I had scrounged from scrap at Calshot was defective after all. Captain Swaffer was not amused and told me in no uncertain terms that if the undercarriage had collapsed on take off, he might have been hurt and of course he was right. It became obvious to me that the sooner I took my Austin Whippet away from Hamble, the better it would be for all concerned.

The nearest place to go was the small aircraft engineering firm of F. G. Miles at Shoreham, near Brighton. I contacted him and he agreed to take my Austin Whippet, examine it, and report on the work to be done in order to get a C of A. Consequently I bought some new bungie and repaired the undercarriage suspension. Then on a fine weekend I left Hamble for Shoreham. All went well for about twenty miles, then the engine laboured and lost power. There was no alternative but to land on a convenient field.

It was somewhat upsetting to find myself with no money in the bank, only a few shillings in my pocket, sitting in an immobile aeroplane in a field belonging to some farmer or landlord whom I did not know and now, after a few minutes, surrounded by schoolchildren asking awkward questions. I must have sat there for half an hour in desperation, so still in despair, I decided to have a go at getting airborne again. No chocks and no brakes, I had to be careful swinging the prop, but she started first time and so I was off. The engine lost power again after another fifteen minutes, but by then being very near Tangmere I was able to put in there. My RAF friends came to my aid and agreed to 'fix it' with the CO for me to leave the Austin Whippet there until the following weekend. They also undertook to fit the larger oil pump which, fortunately, I had brought with me. They arranged my journey back to Calshot. Next weekend I arrived at Shoreham without incident.

Mr F. G. Miles was interested primarily in his prototype 'Martlet' light aeroplane which was already flying. He gave me a very cordial welcome and we agreed to keep in touch. Back at Calshot, the flying boat course over, I was told that I had been posted to 202 Squadron in Malta. A posting which I have never regretted.

Mr Miles wrote to me in Malta and told me the naked truth. Two cylinders of the engine had cracked, due to overheating. The Civil Aviation Authority required that at least two of the steel tubes be sawn through and examined to see whether there was rust within. He also recommended that the fabric on the wings, fuselage and tailplane be renewed. The inevitable had come, and without any funds to ensure its future, I had to bow to it.

On my behalf, Mr Miles sold the aeroplane, which I believe was the last Austin Whippet still flying, for £15. It was hung outside a cinema in Brighton to advertise *Hell's Angels* and I assume it went to a scrap-yard after that.

If only I could have afforded £100 to obtain the C of A and better still if I could have fitted a Genet engine, then in production by Armstrong Siddeley in Coventry, the machine would have been in service for several years longer and may have finished its life in a museum instead of the scrap-yard.

I flew it for only a short time, not more than twenty hours, but was impressed by its ability to land and take off from very restricted places, the ease of handling and the feeling of sturdiness in its construction. I never tried aerobatics, but am sure that it would have mastered them with alacrity. In short, it was a most remarkable aeroplane, designed and built ten years before its time.

CHAPTER IV

Malta 1929-31

So at last after many years of class-rooms, timetables and exams and after fourteen years under instruction, I was free to do and say what I liked, subject only to RAF discipline which was fairly lax in those days, and my own conscience which developed within me during those years of education. I was never ambitious and knew my limitations, but somehow good things came my way, even in Malta.

The unit to which I was posted was No.202 Flying Boat Squadron based at Calafrana. We had trained on flying boats at Calshot but the Air Ministry would not order any for No.202 Squadron until a prototype proved that it could fly 1,000 miles with an adequate reserve of fuel. This is approximately the distance from Plymouth to Gibraltar, from Gibraltar to Malta and from Malta to Aboukir (Egypt). In the meantime we had to make do with seaplanes. These were Fairey III Ds designed for the RNAS in 1917 to operate on wheels from aircraft carriers and airfields or on floats from the water. They had a very steep angle of glide which made every descent seem like a dive-bomber attack. The pilot was encased in a cage of bracing wires so did not wear a parachute. In 1930 our Squadron was re-equipped with Fairey III Fs which were a great improvement, both in looks and aerodynamics, and the pilot could wear a parachute, but basically much the same, with a crew of three, convertible from seaplane to land plane and a Napier Lion engine.

Six of our aircraft went on a cruise of the Eastern Mediterranean in 1930, the route being Fort Agusta (Sicily) Corfu, Athens, Mirabello (Crete), Sollum and Aboukir (Egypt). In 1931 six of our aircraft went on a longer cruise up the Nile to Khartoum. I was privileged to be on both these cruises — in 1930 as the pilot leading the formation with the Station Commander on board, and in 1931 as navigator in the Squadron Commander's aircraft.

Our daily working routine in Malta was not very arduous. In summer the morning parade was at 6 a.m. but only a few officers were expected to take part and the working day would end at noon in the bar of the Officers' Mess. In winter it was much the same except that the parade was at 8 a.m. and we had two hours on duty during the afternoon. Although all of us had certain extra responsibilities — I was Sports Officer — our main interest was flying. We were given some task to perform such as air gunnery, which meant firing two drums of ammunition from a Lewis gun mounted on a scarf ring over the centre cockpit. There were no forward firing guns in these aircraft.

It was however some achievement to fire two drums of ammunition from a Lewis gun because they seldom shot more than ten rounds before jamming, and changing the drums in the slipstream was not easy. Another enigma was the choice of a target because there was no air firing range. I often took a squirt at a seagull but never hit one. Similarly bombing exercises were a matter of choosing one's own target for practice bombs. A properly equipped bombing range became available in 1931.

When we had an adequate supply of old tennis balls we would aim these at the pinnace which patrolled the bay while flying was in progress. It was under the command of one of our officers who had served with the Merchant Navy; he was tall, handsome and dignified and took great pride in observing all nautical conventions but he was the bull's-eye for our tennis balls. Although he was seen to duck once or twice I don't think he was ever hit.

When the Fleet was in port some twenty ships, big and small, and some twenty thousand officers, petty officers and ratings were there to entertain and be entertained, and believe me, when the Royal Navy decides to give a party it is no ordinary one. The aircraft carriers with spacious upper decks, hangar decks and lower decks could reproduce anything from a village green in seventeenth century England to a scene in Montmartre in 1900. The only items missing were young lady guests. There were of course the wives and daughters of officers based in Malta but no hotel where independent young ladies could book in or even families come on a visit. In short there were too many boys and not enough girls at these excellent parties. That is where the 'Fishing Fleet' comes in.

The purpose was to redress the balance and the underlying motive was not always appreciated. Miss K was the proprietor of a hostel in Sliema where she accommodated young ladies from the UK who might enjoy a month or two in a male surplus community. She ruled her flock with a rod of iron and there was no scope for scandal under her roof. She accepted the fact that her guests had marriage in mind and this is not to be condemned. She saw that they became members of the

Sliema Club, which included the Tigne bathing rocks and also the more exclusive Marsa Club. Thus they could swim, dance, play tennis, golf and even polo. She also made sure that they were invited to all the best parties and dances.

They were so well groomed and escorted that we young RAF officers wondered how it was they had no high-water mark or Plimsoll line when they reposed and exposed themselves on the rocks. They must have found somewhere to lie in the sun in the nude and it could not be far away because they had no transport, so we decided to send out a photo recce. We were obliged to take photos and could choose our own targets, and decided that 11 a.m. would be the best time because by noon pink gin would be served at the Sliema Club and after that tennis or lying on the rocks.

Two seaplanes took part in the operation, each with a crew of three; namely pilot, navigator (who was also bomb aimer and photographer) and the NCO wireless operator. I was not detailed for duty that morning.

The formation took off at 10.45 and secrecy was enforced in the Officers' Mess. The WT operators were told to keep WT silence. Having flown north to gain height the formation approached Sliema from the north-east at 500 feet and 80 m.p.h. to find their target. This did not take long because intelligence reports proved to be most reliable. It was the flat roof of Miss K's hostel and about twelve girls were basking there in the sun. Meanwhile these girls became aware that something unusual was happening and when the formation returned in line astern to take photos they were already in full flight seeking cover. The films were duly developed at base but only two gave recognizable evidence to prove our theory. One was of 'The Chocolate Shape' and the other of 'The Snottie's Delight'. It seems these two girls refused to panic. The two prints were pinned on the notice-board in the Sliema Club that evening but higher authority decreed that they be taken down at once and from then on aircraft whether on wheels or on floats were forbidden to fly over Sliema at under 1,000 feet.

In Malta during this time there were several persons of international fame and fortune. The ever popular and respected Lord Louis and Lady Mountbatten and also the amusing and unconventional antics of David Niven and his friend Trubshaw of the Highland Light Infantry. Then there was Flight Lieutenant F. V. West, the adjutant at Calafrana. He lost a leg and was awarded the Victoria Cross in France in 1918 and was and is the most obstinate and determined character one could wish to meet. He was the Air Attaché to the British Legation in Berne during the Second World War, so the few POWs who were clever enough and lucky enough to escape from Germany and enter Switzerland were directed to his office. After the war he was appointed Overseas Manager of the Rank Organization and promoted the world-wide distribution of the film of the Coronation, a great international success.

Freddie and his attractive and vivacious wife Wynne made it their task to befriend newcomers to Calafrana and a few weeks after I arrived they gave a party in their home to celebrate my twenty-first birthday. I am one of many who still share a deep affection for both of them and long may it last. In spite of his affliction Freddie kept up his flying on both the III D and the III F although he had difficulty in getting into the pilot seat of the former.

I was appointed 'Sports Officer' at Calafrana which included a small number of RAF personnel at Halfar, the airfield where the Fleet Air Arm kept and operated their aircraft and an even smaller number based at the RAF Headquarters in Valetta. Our total was between six and seven hundred, the Army had one battalion and supporting forces and were about 1,500 and the Navy many more when the Fleet was in. No wonder we came in third in all inter-service competitions. I took my orders from Freddie and he told me that this situation would soon be remedied.

He was a close friend of several officers on the staff of Air Commodore Forbes the AOC and told them the problem and possibly suggested the solution. No doubt his friend spoke to the AOC, who wrote to the officer in charge of records at Insworth near Gloucester to explain the problem and ask that when the next draft of NCOs and airmen was sent to Malta it should include some athletes, some footballers, and some swimmers.

The result was that we became runners-up in the inter-services football competition and we won the athletics championship. One of the new arrivals, I cannot remember his name for certain but think it was Corporal Charlie Lang, could win any race from 440 yards to five miles and was prepared to run two races on any afternoon.

Occasionally when atmospheric conditions were right we could see Mount Etna in the evening, silhouetted against the northern sky. From the air it could be seen on most days flying at 5,000 feet and above. The crater of Mount Etna is 11,000 feet high and 130 miles from Malta. It is the highest volcano in Europe and probably the most active one.

I was taking an evening stroll with Professor Read, the Education Officer at Calafrana when we saw the silhouette. We were both entitled to local leave and we agreed to have a go at climbing Mount Etna. Having consulted books and maps we came to certain conclusions, namely:

(I) There was no road up to the crater (one was built by Mussolini later on).

(II) There is an observatory there, built by the British garrison in Sicily during the Napoleonic Wars. The stone for this building was probably carried up on mule back.

(III) There are two hundred or more subsidiary craters, all of which have been active at one time or another.

(IV) The main crater was about two miles in diameter but changes after eruptions.

(V) The snow line is usually about 6,000 feet up.

We thought it odd we found no record of servicemen from Malta having attempted this not very dangerous yet very interesting expedition before.

In the workshop we made two pairs of crampons which we reckoned would be necessary above the snow line if the surface was frozen hard. It was! I also made a pair of skis which were not necessary and would have been dangerous to use. These items of equipment were not made from any approved design but from memory and imagination. We packed our warm clothes and rations into our haversacks and embarked in the good ship *Knight of Malta* late one night, bound for Sicily. Several friends including Freddie and Wynne came to see us off and we had a good laugh together, particularly at our 'Garage Rat' skis and crampons.

Next morning we came ashore in Syracuse and took a bus to Catania where we booked in for one night, and went in search of more information on Mount Etna. I found that the local dialect was much nearer my own brand of Spanish than the correct Italian spoken in Rome and Milan, so language was no problem.

We learned that it was not unusual for visitors to climb the volcano, that it would take two days to get up to the cone of the crater but we could come down in one. The starting point must be the village of Adrano, where we should hire a guide with the key to the all-important wooden hut on the snow line where we would spend the night.

Next morning we took the local bus to Adrano, booked in at the primitive village hotel for three nights, found our guide and agreed to start at 8 a.m. next morning. Everybody was most friendly, except the fleas, but we had them in Malta too.

The climb up to the hut was a gentle walk uphill, first through cultivated fields and vineyards then olive groves and orchards and finally pine trees. It took six hours so left plenty of time to decide on our plans for next day.

At 3 a.m. we started implementing the plans because it would be a marvellous experience to see the crater before dawn, which was at 7 a.m. Moonlight and snow gave us the tactical approach, aided by the crampons which we put on when full snow coverage prevailed. Our strategic approach was the initiative of our guide, and we reached the observatory at 6 a.m. We had passed many of the smaller craters or cones and now there were small geysers sending steam four or five feet into the air and a strong smell of sulphur everywhere. The observatory was much smaller than we expected and was not manned but was visited by officials to collect data on the volcano and on wind and weather, etc.

The cone of the main crater rose at a steep angle from where we stood and with limited visibility appeared to be very symmetrical. We began to climb, not exactly on all fours but with our hands near the warm ash to keep balanced, and the advent of dawn brought fog. Our guide said that the fog or cloud would clear soon but it would be unwise to go on any further until then. We did not know how far we were from the rim of the crater so agreed to wait. After some twenty minutes we were cold, the opportunity of seeing the crater in darkness had gone and we were still in cloud so down we went and back to Adrano. We had not fulfilled the total purpose of our local leave but we did climb Mount Etna and then did some touring of Taormina, Catania and Syracuse before embarking on our return in the good ship *Knight of Malta*.

CHAPTER V

The Flying Instructor

In my last term at Cranwell the cadets were told that only those who specialized could expect promotion to higher rank. Except for Doctors and Chaplains there were no semi-independent branches within the RAF as there are today, which accepted only those of their own trade and training and had their own promotion structures. We could apply to specialize in several subjects, such as photography, armaments or signals, and if the applicant were selected he would go to University, usually Cambridge, for two years of higher education and, provided he passed his exams, come back into the main stream of General Duties officers with one year antedated for promotion. I applied for higher education in navigation and engineering but I knew my chances were nil.

There were four short navigation courses every year, which included the flying boat course, and there were only two officers each year selected for the advanced navigation course known as 'Big N'. Thus, even if I passed out top of the flying boat course, which I did not, the chance of selection for 'Big N' was two to one against. In engineering and other technical subjects, the choice went in favour of those young and often brilliant officers who had been chosen to progress to commissioned rank from their Apprentice Schools, via Cranwell.

I was very happy in Malta and resigned to a limited career when, to my surprise, I was told that I had been selected for the next 'Flying Instructor' course at the Central Flying School, Wittering. I was surprised because I did not know flying boat pilots went there.

On arrival at CFS we, the aspiring graduates, found that the instructors were much of the same vintage as ourselves, and had recently passed the course with distinction. My instructor had been a cadet with me at Cranwell in the same term.

We also learned that however brilliantly we might fly, any sloppiness in general conduct, discipline, manners, etc., would be scored against the culprit in the final count. I discovered for the first time, that those of us who qualified as 'A' category instructors would benefit by one year antedated for promotion. There were about fifteen pupils on the course and the usual award for the 'A' category was two, so competition was severe, but the challenge was there and I decided to be a good boy for the next three months.

Having been greeted by my instructor I was introduced to my co-pilot Lieutenant Rasananda from Siam, now Thailand. He was small but well proportioned, intelligent and extremely jolly and friendly and we got on very well. Our instructor, I will refer to him as 'L', explained the routine.

Each morning he would take one and then the other of us up for an hour or so. Then, during the afternoon we would fly together to check and practise on one another. This left time for solo flights and flying the more advanced operational aircraft because all our instructional flying would be done on Avro 504 Ns (Lynx Avros). The first few weeks would be dedicated to improving the accuracy of our flying and ironing out faults which may have developed during our squadron life. Some of us, and I was one, would be obliged to perform aerobatics for the first time. Then we would be introduced into the mystery of CFS 'patter' which meant the instructor explaining to the pupil during each manoeuvre what he was doing and why he was doing it. There was a faintly concealed standard 'patter' but 'L' made it clear that we should look upon it to mould with our own speech and personality. At the end of the course the Chief Flying Instructor would fly with each one of us and make the final assessment of our capability.

I enjoyed all this and took a special delight in prompting Rasananda into using words that he could not pronounce, such as 'aeroplane', 'parallel' and 'horizontal'. There would be loud splutters down the speaking tube and he would end up with a friendly little giggle.

Towards the end of the course there was a dance in the Officers' Mess and the officers under instruction (i.e. graduate aspirants) were each expected to introduce a lady partner to the community. I chose to take my sister Clare. She was in her early twenties, good looking and very good company, but I was apprehensive that she might drop a 'clanger' at this delicate stage of my career. We entered the ante-room together and were received by the CFS Commandant 'Straight Bat' Maltby and his wife. Then Clare said in front of everybody "Now Toby, I would like to meet a Wind Conductor or an Air Commode." Of course, the titles of RAF ranks are still an enigma to everyone not linked closely to our service and we know full well that they are abused, misused and to the outside world bear little relationship to the duties performed and are also quite a mouthful. However, I did fear that this remark by Clare would mean a minus on my score sheet!

Just then I heard the soft voice of Jerry Livock speaking to Clare; "I am a Wing Commander, may I have the pleasure of this dance?" He was a well-known cricketer at that time and was at CFS on a refresher course. Several days later I was told that I had been awarded an 'A' category which put me one step ahead of the brilliant cadets who had been with me at Cranwell and were now at University — no doubt thanks to Clare!

Having passed my preliminary exam for a Spanish interpretership I was now entitled to spend two months in Madrid at HMG's expense so I took the opportunity to do this before being posted to a flying training unit of one kind or another.

When I returned I was posted to No. 2 FTS at Digby in Lincolnshire. This was a wooden hut station and not very comfortable. Pupils and instructors shared the same ante-room in the Officers' Mess and this was not popular with the more seasoned instructors who never felt relaxed, so took every opportunity to go out pub crawling. They had been in service in many countries, the Middle East, the Far East and India and were pleasant and interesting company, never lacking in humour. I went with them to the pubs!

I was in 'D' Flight instructing the senior term of trainees flying Armstrong Whitworth Atlas aircraft which equipped the Army co-operation squadrons at that time. It was then that I crashed for the first time. What a harsh word that is, later to be known as a 'prang' or 'wizard prang' but these latter words had not yet found their way into the Concise Oxford Dictionary. Anyhow, I have had two prangs and this is how the first one happened. The second was in Hong Kong about twenty years hence so I will describe it later on. Both were entirely my own fault.

I was on a low flying exercise demonstrating the skill of hedge-hopping and contour chasing when my pupil screamed, "Look out Sir!" through the speaking tube; almost immediately we were plunging through a mass of foliage branches, bird's nests and all the other secret treasures which a large tree contains and gives up only reluctantly. I had planned my immediate route through a gap between two rows of trees, about seventy yards apart, but had not noticed that one tree stood alone in the middle of the gap.

The dual controil Atlas had two cockpits, the pupil being in front in the proper place and the instructor in a rear cockpit adapted for his role, from space designed for the observer. His forward view was to some extent limited by the configuration of the aircraft. I never made this an excuse for my elementary 'boob'. However the Atlas was a very stalwart aeroplane and we came out of the other side of the tree still airborne. True, the propeller had been broken off, so the engine could give us plenty of revs but not get us places. The plane landed in a ploughed field, ran over the rough surface for about fifty yards, where it came to a ditch and hedge, the wheels sank into the ditch and the fuselage containing my pupil and myself somersaulted slowly over and finished upside down just beyond the hedge. Neither of us was hurt but I was extremely ashamed.

There was only one other instructor at Digby who was an ex-Cranwell cadet and that was Bobby Stowell. We had been there together but he was two terms senior to me. The other instructors held short service commissions and were due for retirement so when, in September of 1933 Digby was closed down, Bobby and I were posted to Cranwell.

There he was given command of 'B' Flight equipped with Atlas aircraft and I was posted to his flight as one of the instructors. We were accommodated in the Officers' Mess and settled down for a while. In July 1934 I was promoted to Flight Lieutenant and given command of 'C' Flight equipped with Avro Tutor aircraft which were a great improvement on the antiquated 504N. Also, Bobby and I were appointed Cadet Wing Officers and allocated a flat in the new building.

Although it was an honour to be selected, there were certain inherent obligations as well as perks. We dined in Mess with the cadets four nights each week and were on parade most mornings. Also we were given other duties and mine was teaching elementary navigation to the two junior term cadets in the class-room. However the perks were there too. The flat I shared with Bobby Stowell had two large bedrooms, a comfortable sitting-room and all mod cons and a batman. We enjoyed also the use of the staff ante-room which was adjacent to the main entrance of the building and comfortably furnished, and was blessed with landscape oil paintings on the wall which were loaned to the college by the Tate Gallery.

One cold and frosty morning the aircraft had been taken out of hangars and lined up ready for the half-hour run up flying prior to the arrival of the cadets, but as happens in Lincolnshire from time to time a blanket of fog rolled in and obscured everything. Visibility was reduced to ten feet and even the birds were walking, not flying. In the flight office we wanted something funny to do during the next hour or so, by which time the fog would have gone, so we planned a little expedition to acquire one of 'D' Flight's aeroplanes. They were next to us equipped also with Tutors and each flight had its own hangar. We took with us a hand compass and a tape measure and groped our way through the fog, from one aircraft to the next, until we reached the twelfth one where we turned through 90° to look for the Tutor at the end of 'D' Flight's line. There were four of us on the expedition and we knew from experience that an Avro Tutor could be manhandled very simply with two lifting the tail plane and steering and two pushing on the leading edges of the wings. We found our prize, groped our way back and hid it in a dark corner of our hangar to await events. The fog cleared and flying got under way when an emissary arrived from 'D' Flight. One of their Tutors was missing and maybe it had been parked, by mistake, with ours. We went outside and counted twelve Tutors on our line and eleven on 'D' Flight's line. No, there had been no one in the air when the fog rolled in; the emissary left but I was becoming somewhat concerned that events might become serious, so I telephoned Flt. Lt. Inglis who commanded 'D' Flight and told him how naughty we had been and we would return his Tutor at once. He was very relieved and told me he had not reported the loss of one Tutor to higher authority because the folks upstairs would never believe that an aeroplane could disappear just like that. We agreed that there would be no recriminations.

CHAPTER VI

Peru 1934-35

In the autumn of 1934 I was content and comfortable at Cranwell for I was a Flight Commander, Cadet Wing Officer and shared a flat in the new building. Then, out of the blue, I was posted to Eastchurch for a short armament course prior to joining an RAF mission to Lima, Peru.

King Edward VII's titles were King of Great Britain and Ireland, Defender of the Faith, Emperor of India, etc. etc. He was known in South America as 'El Pacificador' and in Europe was sometimes referred to as 'Edward the Peacemaker'. When the South American countries decided to separate from Spain, early in the nineteenth century, they could never agree on their respective frontiers and eventually invited Edward VII to arbitrate. He and his advisers made a good job of it and most of their recommendations were confirmed and remain today. There have been however, one or two hiccups and one of these is the boundary between Colombia and Peru.

During the discussions Colombia claimed access to the River Amazon — why not? Was it not from present day Colombian territory that Orellana was the first to navigate the Amazon 3,000 miles from west to east. Although that expedition was in 1541-2, Colombia either won or was unopposed in a bid for a port on the banks of the Amazon. A couple of straight lines were drawn across the map over territory still unexplored and mostly inaccessible rain forest, to converge on a small strip of the river known as Leticia. It is here that the Peruvian, Colombian and Brazilian boundaries meet.

Some 200 miles up river from Leticia is the town of Iquitos, well into Peruvian territory. It was visited by ocean-going ships from Europe, exported tropical produce and imported manufactured goods and other essentials. In fact Europe was much closer to Iquitos in journey time than Lima or Bogota.

Sr Vigil owned a sugar plantation on the banks of the Amazon. His two sons were at school in England and he traded his produce and bought his supplies in Iquitos. All was serene until one day a gunboat arrived flying the Colombian flag. It had come 5,000 miles from

Cartagena in the Caribbean and claimed Leticia belonged to Colombia and that Sr Vigil was obviously trespassing. Sr Vigil was turned out and the gunboat, left a small garrison on his property and headed downstream for home. He was not inactive. When he arrived in Iquitos he gathered his friends around him and recruited a small expedition to go to Leticia to evict the Colombian garrison which they did without a shot being fired by either side.

When the news arrived in Lima and Bogota it became a matter of national pride. I do not remember whether war was declared but all the ingredients were there and both Peru and Colombia began to buy arms. An army battle was not possible because Equador, with its high mountains and great forests came between them. A sea battle was not possible because the Peruvian Navy was in the Pacific and the Colombian Navy was in the Atlantic. Like Tweedledee and Tweedledum they agreed to have a battle, but where? In the air of course, but that too would be difficult.

Both ordered aircraft from the four countries then able to supply them, namely, USA, France, Italy, and the UK. Some of these orders specified floats for use on the rivers east of the Andes, where there were no airfields. Quantities of ancillary supplies such as spares, guns, arms and bombs were also ordered. It was at this stage that the Peruvian President, General Benavidez, asked the British Government to appoint an RAF mission to organize, supervise and train the CAP (i.e. the Peruvian Air Force). The British Government agreed and selected Group Captain Smyth Piggot to go to Lima in advance to assess the situation and make recommendations.

His first recommendation was that all new aircraft and equipment should be put into storage except that needed for cadet training. Next, he recommended that a Cadet School be established on a permanent basis and his third and most important recommendation was that five RAF officers should be seconded to the mission as instructors with specified responsibilities.

During their frequent conversations, the President told Smyth Piggot that Colombia had recruited thirty US mercenary pilots to fly newly acquired aircraft. Would he recruit a similar number of British pilots to fly for Peru? With great diplomacy, Smyth Piggot explained that dark clouds were hovering over Europe with the emergence of Mussolini and Hitler, so Britain needed every trained airman to remain at home in case of war. He concluded by suggesting that he might also recruit thirty mercenary pilots to join the CAP. How right he was.

Shortly after this conversation Italy invaded Abyssinia and we were close to war so the mission to Peru was cancelled and Smyth Piggot recalled. However, bearing in mind that I had just arrived in Lima and the Peruvian Government had paid for my journey and expenses, the Air Ministry conceded that I should remain, on my own, for one year only.

Las Palmas was the main base for the CAP, and it was here that the Cadet School was established. It also contained workshops, storage hangars and a small area for civil aviation. There were two grass/earth runways, each about 600 yards long and rather bumpy. The school was called Jorge Chaves in memory of a Peruvian pioneer aviator who was the first to fly across the Alps.

The CAP appointed Colonel Raguz to be Superintendent and his assistant Commandante Washburn. There were to be four sections, viz:
(1) Primary Training.
(2) Fighter and Aerobatics.
(3) Bomber, armaments and navigation.
(4) Army co-operation and reconnaissance.
Four instructors were appointed, viz:
Section 1 — Captain Alvares (CAP)
Section 2 — Captain Bianchi (Italy)
Section 3 — H.M.P. (RAF)
Section 4 — Donald Kesler (USA)

Apart from myself, two of these appointments were of interest. Firstly, Luigi Bianchi — he was a Captain in the Regia Aeronautica (i.e. Royal Italian Air Force) and seconded to the Caproni Company as test pilot in Peru. He was and is a flamboyant character and eventually became a four-star General in the NATO forces after the Second World War. In spite of the near war situation which existed in Europe between UK and Italy, we resolved to be friends and oblivious to the provocations of our Peruvian hosts, who even advocated (in fun, I believe) an aerial combat between us, which were mutually ignored.

Luigi had a motor car and I did not. We both lived in Miraflores, a suburb of Lima about five miles from Las Palmas. He took me there in his car every morning on the way to breakfast with our Peruvian friends, and we often discussed the situation in Europe without acrimony.

Donald Kesler had recently married an attractive Peruvian lady. He had no commitments to the US Government nor to any aircraft manufacturer. He was trained in the US Army Air Force on a limited service basis and after that, according to his own intriguing accounts, he became another maverick pilot in Latin America flying aircraft sometimes belonging to himself and sometimes to somebody else. He denied all knowledge of the load he carried, maybe guns, maybe drugs or strawberries and cream! In those days frontiers could be crossed and there were no national airports or controls. He joined the CAP in order to settle down with his wife and lead a more stable and mundane existence.

We all wore the CAP uniform and were given the rank of Captain. Caesar Alvares was the doyen and sat at the head of the table at meals. He was intelligent and quiet and we all enjoyed his company and respected his authority.

There were no serious accidents during that year, but a few minor misadventures. One morning Caesar returned to base with his cadet pupil and decided to do a loop at about 1,500 feet in full view of all of us. Either he had forgotten to strap himself in or he had done it wrongly — but he fell out. Fortunately his GQ parachute opened and his pupil landed the Morane safely. Sad to tell, Caesar was killed in a road accident soon after I left Peru.

We four instructors were allowed, and indeed encouraged, to fly each other's aircraft, provided we obtained the permission of Caesar and the other instructor concerned. We took full advantage of this privilege and a great deal of swapping went on.

Next came the allocation of aircraft. Alvarez of Section One was given four Morane Primary Trainers. These were sturdy little French high wing monoplanes with a performance akin to the Avro Tutor of that time. The landing speed was a trifle higher, but they managed to cope well with the bumpy airfield surface.

Luigi Bianchi was the most fortunate. He got four Caproni fighters with which he was very familiar. These biplanes were a delight to see and to fly. In performance they resembled the Gloster Gauntlet of the RAF and were powered by Bristol Mercury engines, built in Italy under licence. Each had two Vickers guns firing through the propeller via a Constantinesco hydraulic interrupter.

He had also the use of a Caproni advanced trainer which was unarmed and intended primarily for exhibition flying. Its engine was a powerful one, adapted for inverted flying. Probably it did not belong to the CAP at all, but to the Caproni Company as it was the only one of its kind in Peru.

Donald Kesler made do with a Curtiss Falcon, a Lockheed Corsair and two Henriot two-seater advanced trainers, and since he did not need any armaments for his role, he was quite content that he and his cadets should co-operate in exercises with the Peruvian Army.

I was expected to teach bombing, armaments and navigation. To me that meant practice bombs, a bombing range, bomb sights that I understood, guns that I had studied, an air to ground firing range, and an air to air firing range. The last was impossible to achieve, but with the help of my cadets we managed quite a lot by improvisation. I would have dearly liked one Fairey Gordon in my section. It carried all the armaments which I knew and had used in the RAF but for reasons which I will explain later, this was not possible.

The small practice bombs used by the RAF are well shaped and give off a white puff of smoke on impact. They are made of steel with a detonator and a filler of stannic. The CAP would not buy these in quantity because they reckoned they could make them in Peru. So they could, and did make half a dozen or so very well, but the cost was much too high, so we had to improvise. My cadets suggested they could make practice bombs of the right shape and size out of clay mixed with a small quantity of cement. A piece of thick wire would be looped and buried in the mixture to give the essential suspension to the bomb rack of the aircraft. We went ahead with this idea and the cadets had to make their bombs before they could drop them. They agreed to this with enthusiasm. Although the 'trail angle' was doubtful, the clay/cement bombs enabled the cadets to use the bombing range which we improvised also. The key to success was that the bombs, on impact with the sand salt flats on which the range was built, gave up small columns of dust, so a bearing could be taken.

There was, at that time, a substantial area of disused land on the coast not far from Las Palmas. It belonged to nobody, was remote from any dwellings or farms, and the surface was firm enough for our aircraft to land and take off. We made a target by whitewashing some large stones. Two control huts were made from aircraft packing cases, and two radial bearing tables from some ancient Aldis gun sights which we found in store. These were mounted on circular wooden discs marked off in degrees of the compass. There were no field telephones available to pass bearings from the secondary hut to the main control hut in which the fall of the bomb was plotted. We overcame this by using a board with large numerals on pegs like a cricket score-board. The board was read with binoculars from the main hut and the fall of each bomb plotted accordingly. So we had a bombing range as well as practice bombs.

The air to ground range was easy. A circle was made on the sandy beach and the number of bullet marks on the sand recorded. Luigi's Caproni fighters joined in and there was quite a healthy competition between his cadets and mine.

My section had been allocated three Potez medium bombers. These were high wing monoplanes with corrugated dural fuselages and wing coverings. In performance they were similar to the Hawker Hart, but were larger. They were easy to fly and presented no problem in that respect, at Las Palmas. However they could not be adapted to take the Course Setting Bomb Sight (Wimpris) which I was teaching in the class-room, nor were they equipped with a light series bomb rack which could carry our home-made practice bombs. Therefore, much to the delight of my cadets, they were used on navigation exercises up and down the coast and for formation flying. We had also two Hanriot advanced trainers each fitted with one Darne machine-gun. These guns not only had a higher rate of fire than the Vickers, but were much more reliable. We used these Hanriots for air to ground firing exercises and for commuting between Las Palmas and the bombing range.

Our greatest asset was a Curtiss Falcon. In performance it was similar to the Fairey Fox Mk I which equipped No. 12 Squadron of the RAF based at Andover. Indeed the engine was the same, the Curtiss D 12. However, what pleased me more, it had a light series bomb rack which could take our home-made practice bombs and was far more reliable than the one used by the RAF. Also, with a little adaptation, the Wimpris bomb sight was fitted in the floor hatch. This aircraft was used exclusively for practice bombing.

For all this improvisation I was indebted to George Vigil who was in charge of the workshops at Las Palmas and bent over backwards to help me and my cadets.

I have no doubt that the cadets were selected from the higher grades of education. It was a time when glamour went with aviation, more so being a pilot in South America, so there was no lack of applicants and they were intelligent, well groomed, enthusiastic and disciplined. I doubt whether any of them worried much about the controversy with Colombia; they just wanted to become professional aviators.

My concern was that future instruction at Las Palmas was at risk. Having understood a subject, which they did very quickly, the cadets were inclined to progress to something new rather than pursue the original subject in detail.

The only operational squadron of the CAP was based at Chiclayo, about 350 miles north of Lima, and equipped with Caproni heavy bombers. These were high wing monoplanes each powered by a single engine and unlike the other Italian aeroplanes in Peru, they were ugly monsters and underpowered. Nevertheless it was only from Chiclayo that the CAP could, in theory, reach targets in Colombia, overflying Equador. There was also a small unit in Iquitos with half a dozen Curtiss single seater fighters on floats, intended to protect that town from air attack. Finally several light transport planes, Stinston, Fairchild, Travelair, some on floats in eastern Peru, and some on wheels, on the western coast were used for communications.

Many new aircraft were in store both in the hangars at Las Palmas and in warehouses at the port of Lima (Callao). These included substantial replacements for ones already mentioned and several unknown species. For example twelve Nieuport single seater fighters, fearsome looking high wing monoplanes, with twin Darne guns. No one doubted their performance, but their ability to take off and land at Las Palmas was debatable.

Then we come to the UK aircraft; six Fairey Foxes and six Fairey Gordons. The Fox was not the same aeroplane as that which equipped No. 12 Squadron for this one had a metal frame and was powered by a Rolls-Royce Kestrel engine. It had been in competition with the Hawker Hart for RAF contracts but the Hart won and the Fox was sold abroad. It was a favourite with the CAP not only because of its good looks but also because it performed so well at high altitude. Although all six were in storage while I was in Peru, before then the six Foxes, piloted by veteran CAP officers, had flown in formation from Lima to Cuzco, the ancient Inca capital city. The distance is 400 miles and the height of the landing strip 12,000 feet so to cross the summit they must have flown at above 18,000 feet. They returned the same way as they came.

The Fairey Gordon was a derivative of the Fairey III F powered by an Armstrong Siddeley Panther engine. The six Gordons were delivered with floats as well as wheels and were intended for use on the large rivers east of the Andes. In order to get there they would need to take off from the sea, cross the Andes at not less than 16,000 feet and alight at Iquitos on the Amazon or at Pucalpa on the Ucayali river. Another plan was that Gordon floatplanes should be based at one or other of the two big lakes on the mountain plateau, viz. Lake Titicaca (12,000 feet) and Lake Junin (13,000 feet). When such plans, which entailed long range high flying and high altitude take off, became known, the Engineers of Armstrong Siddeley recognized that there was a problem unique in the world of floatplanes. They sent a team to Lima with specially manufactured superchargers designed to meet these conditions. Later on when it became apparent that war with Colombia would not develop, the Gordons were restored to their former boost and spent many useful years on wheels on the coastal airfields of Western Peru.

And so my time in Peru was coming to an end and the school at Las Palmas closed down for holidays. There were still a few weeks to go before my year was up and the CAP suggested that I should see the other face of Peru. A face of huge rivers, swamps and jungle, and to get there I would be taken by motor car over the road and rail summit (16,000 feet) across the high plateau and down the other side. It was a two day journey, much of it on narrow roads carved out of the edge of precipices. The road was so narrow that two vehicles could not pass, so there were up days and down days, but I arrived safely at San Ramon, where there was an airstrip and a Stinston Detrioter waiting for me. San Ramon is on the eastern slopes of the Andes at about 4,000 feet. It is a green and wooded valley, cultivated with coffee, tea and citrus fruits. The only other airstrip east of the Andes was Pucalpa on the river Ucayali about 200 miles north-east of San Ramon, and surrounded by dense jungle.

I stayed at Pucalpa for three days and was given the choice of waiting for a floatplane to arrive from Iquitos or embarking on a river boat to take me there. I opted for the latter and spent five very interesting days on board. Every fifty miles or so we put into the river bank to take on timber which had been stockpiled, to fuel the boilers of the boat. When this happened the heat, humidity and insects were very oppressive but out in midstream I could relax and enjoy the myriad of tropical birds of all colours and the trees and vegetation of all kinds on the banks.

The Ucayali joins the river Maranon a short distance west of Iquitos and from there onwards the combined river becomes the Amazon.

At Iquitos I lodged with the CAP but spent much of my time with the British Vice Consul, Mr Massey. He had been there for twenty years or more and pioneered several tropical products for export to Europe and the USA. While there I was invited by the CAP to fly to Leticia which was now the base for a three nation Commission to decide on the frontiers between Colombia, Peru and Brazil. The Chairman of the Commission was from Brazil and there were delegates from the other two countries. They seemed to get on well together and it was obvious that no war was imminent. After several hours in a friendly atmosphere I returned to Iquitos with my CAP friends. The way back to Lima was by floatplane from Iquitos to Pucalpa and from there, the way I had come.

Before leaving Peru the CAP gave a dinner in my honour and announced that I had been awarded the Peruvian Air Force Cross, which the Foreign Office in London agreed I could wear. My cadets came to see me off in the ship when I left for home. No doubt the same send off was given to Luigi and Don, who left Peru after me.

CHAPTER VII

Filton 1936 — The Impossible Task

On coming back from Peru I was posted to RAF Station Filton to be adjutant to the CO of No. 501 (Bomber) Squadron. This sounded great, because to be adjutant to the CO of an auxiliary squadron had always been a very coveted appointment. Moreover the airfield was shared with the test pilots of the Bristol Aeroplane Company and Bristol Engines Ltd., so there would be new things to see in the world of aviation, almost every day. A flying school used the airfield also, where reserve pilots were trained on Tiger Moths up to the elementary stage, under contract to the RAF.

The countryside very beautiful, the people very friendly, the buildings of the RAF station were brick built and designed for permanent use, but I realized before long that I had been given an impossible task to fulfil.

Filton had been for many years an RAF station with an administrative staff on which units based there or on temporary deployment there, could provide basic necessities. Airmen must be paid, stores must be available and accountable, transport must be provided when required and forms filled in. At Filton this staff was, until my arrival, provided by a Special Reserve Squadron commanded by a Squadron Leader or Wing Commander with eight officers trained and dedicated to their particular duties, but No. 501 City of Bristol Special Reserve Squadron had become an Auxiliary Squadron, so all the officers had been sent away and I was posted there with Flying Officer M. V. M. Clube, who arrived at the same time, to carry on. It was fortunate that 'Club' and I became friends immediately: we shared the same regard for responsibility, the same humour and sense of the ridiculous. We were together later on during the war and still meet now and then. 'Club's' title was 'assistant adjutant' so we set about planning who would take on what. For example:

Station Commander
No. 501 Auxiliary (Bomber) Squadron Commander
Chief Flying Instructor

Chief Ground Instructor
Accountant Officer
Stores Officer
PSI President of Services Institute
PMC President Mess Committee

We did accept with grace that the Doctor who cared for our physical welfare and the Chaplain who cared for our spiritual welfare and the Education Officer who cared for our mental well-being were in local practices and they too were grateful for becoming honorary members of the Officers' Mess. I was alarmed to hear that I was the Commanding Officer of the Mobilization Centre for South-West Britain and the Commanding Officer of the Port Embarkation Unit at Avonmouth. However it turned out that these appointments were a matter of convenience and required no action from me.

Neither 'Club' nor I had any experience in administration and it was apparent that we were being thrown in at the deep end.

I made several appeals to No. 6 Group Headquarters in London but got no sympathy. The answer was always the same, I must recruit more auxiliaries and train them for the job vacancies. And I should go out and get to know the heads of industry in Bristol and the landed gentry in South Gloucestershire to recruit their heirs and successors. Yes, I knew we could recruit pilots from that quarter, indeed we had a few already and with some exceptions they treated Filton as a club where an aeroplane would be available to fly (or not to fly) and the Officers' Mess a place with comfortable chairs where they could bring their friends, enjoy a late night bar service and even bed and breakfast if there was nowhere else to go.

Across the airfield were the premises of the Bristol Aircraft and Bristol Engines factories. From there we could have recruited all the aircrews, groundcrews and administrative personnel we needed, and indeed we received many applications, but they were all in reserved occupations and therefore not eligible.

It seemed to me that the task of establishing a self-supporting unit was impossible and that there would be trouble sooner or later. So I must get the accounts right, well kept and well presented, because unless this were done my integrity would be suspect if and when irregularities occurred. The sum I received for entertainment purposes was £75 p.a. and I discovered a youth who was articled to a firm of chartered accountants in Bristol who agreed to join the squadron as Accountant Officer for £75.

The severe cuts in the number of regular officers at Filton were not entirely reflected when it came to the non-commissioned ranks. Although there were less NCOs and airmen than before we were able to keep aircraft flying and transport running.

When I first went to Filton, No. 501 Squadron was equipped with Westland Wallace aircraft. These were rather large biplanes, intended to replace the Wapiti in service abroad. Soon after, they were replaced by Hawker Hind light bombers.

That summer (1936) the squadron went to camp for two weeks at Donibristle, Fife, Scotland. We took twelve Hinds for the qualified aircrews, a Tiger Moth and an Avro 504N for the three *abinitio* officers who were under instruction. Donibristle was used by the Fleet Air Arm to accommodate men and machines when aircraft carriers were out of commission and in the Rosyth Dockyard.

We had the use of air firing and bombing ranges and there was a permanent staff which provided the basic essentials for a visiting squadron. Summer camp at Donibristle was, for 'Club' and me, a great success. We started with PT before breakfast and some evenings we finished on the last ferry back across the Firth of Forth from Edinburgh. We cemented friendships with large measures of Scottish cement, and we arrived back at Filton on time and a united unit.

In common with all Auxiliary Squadrons, Saturday and Sunday were the busy days when the auxiliaries arrived for training, experience, pay and company. Tuesday and Wednesday were the days off for 'Club' and me and usually we went our own ways but sometimes joined our colleagues in a crawl from Iron Acton, through Chipping Sodbury (13 pubs) on to Tetbury and then to Malmesbury where we sucked a lemon each for half-time. The return was more painful for 'Club' than for me because his beautiful and talented wife was waiting for him with a rolling pin. My abode was only a number on the door of my bedroom in the Officers' Mess, where I was comparatively safe.

On two or three occasions we suffered visits by the Air Officer Commanding No. 6 Group whose Headquarters were in London. He was quite oblivious to our problems, demanded a parade on such occasions, and on one ordered all the airmen to lift up their feet so he could examine the soles of their boots.

It was in mid-December 1936 that I received a written order to report immediately to DDAFL at the Air Ministry. This is the branch which dealt with Air Attachés, both ours overseas and theirs over here. The letters stand for Deputy Director Air Foreign

Liaison. I was required to go to Spain and the sooner the better. A replacement adjutant would be sent to No. 501 (Bomber) Squadron at Filton and how soon could I get there? We agreed on one week and I went back to Filton.

There I concentrated not on my packing, nor my tickets and passports but on handing over certificates, in accordance with King's Rules and Regulations and Air Council Instructions. 'Club' and I got LAC Arisgog, the orderly room clerk and also the clerk whom the Territorial Association so kindly provided for our benefit to prepare these. There were about fifteen such certificates which I signed as 'handing over' and space was left for the officer 'taking over' to sign.

I discovered later that a Cranwell contemporary of mine, Robin Hood, flew in one day to Filton and claimed to be the adjutant designate, but when asked to sign the certificates he went back to whence he came and was not seen again for some time.

With regard to No. 501 City of Bristol Bomber Squadron my departure was a turning point in its fortunes. 'Club' became the Commanding Officer. He had served seven years of his short service commission and joined Mardon Son and Hall, a subsidiary of Imperial Tobacco, so he was a genuine auxiliary officer. Also additional administrative support was given to Filton. The Squadron was equipped with Hurricanes in 1939 and became a Fighter Command Squadron in No. 10 Group.

CHAPTER VIII

The Civil War in Spain

Madrid at this time was almost surrounded by the Nationalists. All railways to and from the city had been cut and the only access to the capital was by a diversion on a secondary road that led to the main one to Valencia and the south-east. I had my journey planned for me by the Air Ministry or Foreign Office. First the boat train to Paris, where I called on my immediate superior, the Air Attaché. I never saw him again, but sent copies of my reports and we exchanged letters now and then. I took the night train to Toulouse and a taxi to the airfield. A daily service was flown from there, by a French civil organization, to Barcelona, Valencia and Alicante. The aeroplane carried about fifteen or twenty passengers, I think it was a Breguet, and the service was provided for privileged travellers only.

At Alicante I was met by a uniformed driver of the Scottish Ambulance, with his vehicle. This was a non-political organization financed by charitable donations and subscriptions raised in Scotland and intended to provide medical aid to casualties from both sides. Franco would not allow SA to operate in Nationalist Spain so on occasions there was a spare ambulance to send to one or other of those Mediterranean seaports which were still in use by the Government, to collect supplies and to carry approved passengers.

The driver took me to the hotel used by such passengers and we agreed on the time for an early start on our drive to Madrid. It was a long and bumpy one, the roads were very rough and as we progressed inland the more arid the countryside became. However, we arrived in time for supper, bath and bed. It was a pleasure to greet and be greeted by several members of the domestic staff who had been employed in the Embassy for many years and to remind one another of our acquaintance in 1932 while I was studying in Madrid, for my interpretership.

Next day I was introduced to the diplomatic staff of the Embassy, starting with Sir George Ogilvie Forbes the Chargé d'affaires. The Ambassador accredited to the Spanish Government was Sir Henry Chilton but during the confusion which existed in the early days of the civil war, when it seemed that Franco and the armed forces would take Madrid and enjoy a quick and total victory, the Foreign Office decided that Sir Henry and selected members of his diplomatic staff, should move to Herndaye, just across the border from Spain and in French Basque territory. Sir George and a small staff would remain in Madrid. Sir George assumed the title of Chargé d'affaires.

The daily routine was well established and ten or fifteen of us sat down to simple but adequate meals together, with Sir George. The conversation was open and I learned quite a lot about the local situation. For example, the reason for all the hurry to have an RAF presence in Madrid was to avoid an awkward question in Parliament, to the effect that we should have one there because the capital was being bombed.

Sirens sounded every day but during the few weeks I spent in Madrid, before we moved to Valencia, I never saw one bomb dropped nor one bomber aircraft over the city. However, all my colleagues insisted that bombs had been dropped but probably from Junkers 52 civil aircraft which had been in use in Spain for transport purposes for some time. Small bombs, 50 lbs or less, could be launched through the passenger door, or from an improvised bomb rack. My attention was however focused on the arrival overhead of a substantial number of low wing, single seater (radial engined) fighters, at the same time as the sirens sounded. They flew very fast, and it was apparent that a control and reporting system was now in use. The fighters were Russian and known in Spain as Moscas (Flies), and in my opinion they were flown then by Russian pilots, although later, a conversion unit was formed to train Mosca pilots in Spain.

The ground battle for Madrid took place in the western outskirts of the city where the new university was under construction. It ended in a stalemate with the Nationalists occupying some of the faculty buildings and the Government forces in the others. Skirmishes still happened quite frequently and could be seen from the British hospital on a rising slope overlooking the university area. The hospital continued to receive patients, many from the battlefield, and the Scottish Ambulance was based there under Miss Jacobson. The hospital Matron, Miss Hill, consistently refused to move, and, a large Red Cross and an equally large Union Flag were flown over the hospital building every day.

On the whole the rights and wrongs of the two sides when debated in conversation were in favour of the Nationalists. We saw all around us the persecution of innocent people, because they lived in a society, or belonged to a profession that was no longer allowed to exist. The

Government had lost all authority and the unions ruled the roost, although often fighting between themselves. And yet there was the deeper knowledge that a war in Europe seemed to be inevitable and we were bound to be implicated. Would it be on the side of the Communists or the Fascists? However alike they were in their ends and their means, it was a choice of two evils.

I cannot claim to have seen large numbers of dead bodies in the streets of Madrid, but I did learn the facts of life, which the ordinary citizen had to live with. Let me suggest that Señor A, a member of the CNT, disliked Señor B, because he considered him to be a Fascist or a Capitalist or an Aristocrat, or more likely he owed him 1,000 pesetas which he had no intention of paying back. Señor A would denounce Señor B. The latter would be taken to prison to await the verdict of a standing tribunal, appointed by the Government. The tribunal would find Señor B not guilty of being an enemy of the state and order his release.

This verdict would be regarded by the CNT as an insult, and their boys would be at the prison gate to take Señor B on a coach trip together with several others (*un paseito*) from which they would never return alive. Bodies were picked up by Government lorries in the early morning and taken to a mortuary in Madrid for identification.

Sir George visited these mortuaries on several occasions and counted the corpses. No doubt he reported to the Foreign Office and there were several releases to the press in Britain. Also we were very concerned about the welfare of employees, advisers, acquaintances, etc. who may have been denounced, and were awaiting the verdict of the tribunal. Fortunately the British Consul knew the authorities conducting these tribunals and was told when one of our friends was due to appear. An embassy car with the CD number plates and an accredited member of the staff would be waiting outside the prison with an oversize Union Flag on the bonnet.

There were difficulties of course and perhaps the main one was that many of our friends were eligible for military service, and were guilty of desertion for not enlisting. These would be sentenced by the tribunal to imprisonment, which was a lot safer than being freed from prison and taken for a '*paseito*' into the country by the FIA, the CNT, the UGT, or any one or other of the unions.

The Foreign Office did not allow our Embassy in Madrid to harbour refugees. This was sensible because we may be ordered at short notice, to go elsewhere, so what would become of them? The

Chilean and the Finnish Embassies were reported to have over one hundred refugees each and the problem of feeding them was severe enough but to move them to some, as yet, unknown destination was insuperable. These two countries were not on the 'world stage' but we were. Wherever the Spanish Government went we must go and in early 1937 we made ready for our exit from Madrid to Valencia. We had no permanent refugees, but as usual, some in transit. Those who had not committed crimes against the state were taken, by transport supplied by the Embassy, to one or other of four Mediterranean ports and by ship to Marseilles. These were the sick, women, children and old men. There were others who were obliged to use less conventional means to leave the country. Thus Valencia became the domestic focus of the Spanish Government and of the embassies of the nations most closely involved with affairs in Spain.

I went to Valencia, in advance, to help the consul there prepare accommodation and all the other facilities which would be necessary to enable diplomatic ties between the Spanish Government and the Foreign Office in London to continue without interruption. On arrival I soon discovered what a magnificent job the consul had done already. His name was William Sullivan and later he became Sir William, but we called him Comsomol.

Far from resenting the intrusion into his territory by twenty or more diplomatic staff, he wanted us to occupy as many properties as possible which belonged to British subjects who had left Spain because of the Civil War, and to use these and furnishings for our own well-being. The only stipulation he made was that a notice, printed in Spanish to the effect that the property was under the protection of the British Embassy, was to be displayed at the entrance door. These notices were supplied by the consulate together with a printed Union Flag to stick on also.

Comsomol's immediate concern was to find and make ready a building suitable for the Embassy, with sufficient private accommodation for the Chargé d'affaires and his diplomatic staff and also office space for the attachés, the chancery and a communications centre. I believe it was offered to us by the Government but the place we went to see was ghastly. It had decayed evidence of past pseudo-opulence everywhere, extinct plumbing, inefficient drainage and ancient electric connections. We shook our heads and wondered what to do next, but realized that it was the only site which met the essential conditions so Comsomol decided to recommend it to Sir George.

And so the Embassy was transferred to Valencia from Madrid and shortly afterwards Sir George was recalled to duties elsewhere. I recall that he was appointed British Ambassador in Caracus, Venezuela. We were all sorry to see him go.

His replacement was no longer Chargé d'affaires but accredited with full diplomatic status of Ambassador. In my opinion, shared by others, he was a typical 'Miller of Dee' man, and the camaraderie, which members of the staff had enjoyed in the past, quickly evaporated.

The Royal Navy had a ship lying off the harbour of Valencia and others patrolling the coast between Cartagena and Barcelona and where necessary putting in at one port or another. The main task was to give protection to merchant ships flying the Red Duster, which continued to trade with Spain, sometimes with both sides. The Nationalists had the Spanish Navy under their control, and the Government needed to import raw materials, food and armaments in order to continue the war and feed the people.

The Navy also supplied us with essentials such as petrol and whisky. It was ironic that none of the crew, be they officers, petty officers or ratings were allowed to go ashore at these ports except in a group on duty. For relaxation the ships put in at Palma, Majorca — Franco territory.

One morning I received a telephone call from Colonel Camacho of Air Force Headquarters. He was the link between the Spanish Air Force and foreign attachés, such as myself, and representatives of one kind or another of other countries. He asked me to go to see him in his office, as soon as possible, so we agreed on the time and I went dressed in uniform, which I seldom wore in those days.

He told me that the British Embassy in Madrid had been bombed by the Fascists and that an aeroplane and pilot were at my disposal to take me to Madrid to see the damage. The aeroplane turned out to be a 'Fox Moth', basically a Tiger Moth with an expanded fuselage to take a cabin for three passengers. Fortunately I was the only passenger, and had the cabin to myself. The pilot was in front.

We landed at Alcala de Henares a military airfield about twenty-five miles east of Madrid, on the Guadalajara road. Twenty to thirty Moscas were parked around the perimeter and we were taken through a building with a large room where sinister looking characters, some with beards, were squatting on the floor. I seem to remember, although not certain, that they had snow on their boots.

Some time later I was told that the pilot should have landed at

Barajas, which is now the airport for Madrid, but was then used by light aeroplanes only.

The Embassy was empty, with the veteran care and maintenance staff only. Obviously it had not been hit by a bomb but I was told that a building close by, which had been used by the Embassy as an annexe but was now empty, had been damaged by either a bomb or an artillery shell. I went round to see, and it was evident that the damage was very superficial, and I was of the opinion that it was a shell that hit it. At 13.00 hrs (i.e. 1 p.m.) every day of the week, except Sunday, the Nationalists fired three small shells (probably 7.5 cm) at the Telefonica building. This was the tallest building in Madrid and on the top floor was an observation post from where the Government could overlook the Nationalist positions to the west and particularly the University city. Why these shells were fired with such regularity nobody knew, but a lot of people turned up each day to see. They seldom missed the Telefonica but if one did it would fall and explode in the area where the Embassy was situated.

Two days later the Fox Moth was waiting for me at Barajas and so I went back to Valencia but I shall never know whether this unusual act was one of friendship, of propaganda, or one big joke.

A few weeks later we learned the expected assault on Madrid was imminent and the Nationalists would have four columns marching on the capital, and the fifth column would be the citizens of Madrid who were by now appalled by Communism, the social revolution, and rule by the unions. The western approach was guarded by the International Brigade, well disciplined and either fanatical Communists or those who liked a fight. The eastern approach appeared vulnerable to attack by an Italian Brigade, which was advancing along the main road from Zaragoza. When the Italians were in the vicinity of the town of Guadalajara, they were engaged by a substantial number of 'Ratas'. These were single engined Russian biplanes designed and built for ground attack and had probably assembled at Alcala de Henares for this very purpose. I never knew what their armament was, but I assumed it included machine-guns, rockets and Cooper bombs. The result was devastating. The Italians retreated in disarray and the assault on Madrid was no longer imminent.

Reliable information on the progress of the war was always difficult to obtain. Press reporters would attend the daily briefing and the news for the day was written up on a blackboard. They would be given facilities to write their report, and pass to the censors two or more copies.

Having approved the report, the censor would give the reporter the use of a telephone to contact his newspaper or agency. The censor would monitor the conversation and if the reporter were to deviate from the approved text by one iota he would be cut off. No news agency or newspaper could afford to be without news from Spain in 1937.

Major Richards, the Military Attaché and I met every morning and went through the local newspaper to see if there was anything worthy of a report to our respective bosses in Whitehall. There seldom was, and of course the newspapers in Valencia were subject to the same restrictions as the foreign and international press. One morning, however, he handed me the paper and said, "Here is something for you to get your teeth into." There were two full length pages which dealt exclusively with the air attack on the Italian Brigade near Guadalajara. It gave detail of the number of aircraft engaged, the armaments used and the result on the enemy. We in Valencia knew by listening to the Nationalist radio, that a major attack on Madrid was expected but we had no hint that the attack had been stopped, before it developed, by air power.

I made a quick abbreviated translation and sent this and the two pages of the newspaper to the Air Ministry. All correspondence went by diplomatic bag and we usually handed this over to the Navy unless one of the accredited staff was travelling. Not long after I received from DDAFL a very complimentary letter for having obtained this information and for sending it so quickly. There seemed to be a hidden message which I deciphered later.

The Generals at the War Office and the Air Marshals at the Air Ministry were having their perennial debate on the role of aircraft in a land battle. The soldiers claimed that concentrations of men or supplies were natural targets for the artillery and aeroplanes were needed only to spot for the gunners and for tactical reconnaissance. The airmen responded that in trench warfare that may be so but a future war would be fought with mobile forces and targets well behind the enemy front must be attacked and this could only be done from the air. It is possible that my report had influenced the debate.

So what would happen next in Spain? The Nationalists still called the tune and German aircraft and arms were beginning to arrive with instructors, technicians and aircrews. They chose to test these weapons in the Basque territories on the north coast which had never been sympathetic to Communism and the Social Revolution. All they wanted was an independent Basque state, which included the French Basques, and to speak their own language and practise their religion and exercise their customs. They had believed they were more likely to achieve all this by remaining loyal to the Government than by transferring their allegiance to the Nationalists. The Basques were now isolated and defenceless.

The other theatre of war was the valley of Teruel in the Cuenca hills, south-east of Madrid which led to the Mediterranean coast; to be precise to the town of Sagunto. Should the Nationalists achieve this, Barcelona, the largest city in Spain, would have no communication with Madrid nor with Valencia, Alicante, Almeria and other fertile lands which provided food for the people.

In the summer of 1937 I was ordered to go from Valencia to Bayonne to board a Royal Navy destroyer bound for Bilbao. The plane from Valencia arrived late at Toulouse and I missed my rail connection, so I hired a light aeroplane.

The light aeroplane was a two seater (Caudron I think), and the pilot, a fat and jolly Frenchman. The remarkable feature was that the joy stick was suspended from the roof of the cabin instead of being secured to the cabin floor. It certainly gave much more leg room inside the cabin, and it amused me to see my companion hanging in the cockpit as if he were in a crowded tube train. I suppose in those days every country designed aircraft without much heed to what was happening elsewhere.

We got as far as Pau and it was getting dark so we decided to land there. I continued by taxi and arrived in Bayonne just in time to be taken aboard the destroyer, HMS *Bulldog*. Next morning I was in Bilbao, and went to call on the British Consul General, Mr Stevenson.

He told me that the Basques were unlikely to put up a spirited resistance to the advancing Nationalist army but precautions were being taken to minimize casualties, particularly from air attack. He was supervising the evacuation to the UK of Basque children and the last shipload was due to leave that afternoon escorted by the destroyer *Bulldog*. Would I like to go to the gun emplacement overlooking the approaches to the harbour to see them off? So I spent the afternoon with this very charming and capable man and we agreed on the programme for my visit. It was to include a visit to Santander, some 50 miles west of Bilbao and on my return I would visit a depot where the debris of crashed aircraft was on display. He provided me with a motor car and chauffeur and made it very clear that I must return on schedule to embark on the destroyer because it was her last trip to Bayonne. There were two main purposes for my visit to Santander. The first was to see who was responsible for the sinking of the Spanish battleship *Espania*, a few weeks before. This ship remained loyal to the Government and although old and slow could out-gun the two new cruisers which had defected to the Nationalists. She had sunk outside Santander harbour following an explosion. The other purpose of my visit was to report on any bomb raids. There was another reason which was to visit a family who lived near Santander and had close connections with the UK. Mr Stevenson wanted to know whether they were safe.

Having arrived at Santander, which had once been the seaside resort for the aristocracy, to protect them from the blistering heat of Madrid in summer, I went to the office of the harbour-master who was expecting me, and could not have been more friendly and co-operative. He displayed a chart of the harbour area with two bearings from shore stations of the final resting place of the *Espania*. One shore station was his own headquarters in the harbour and the other was a coastguard observation post on the coast east of the port. I recorded these bearings and declined an offer to keep the Admiralty chart. There was no doubt in my mind that the exact position of the wreck had been established but the 'who and why' remained an enigma, and one open to discussion. It was either a torpedo from a submarine, but in restricted waters that seemed unlikely. I agreed with the harbour-master that it was probably a mine.

Next morning I returned to Bilbao and in the afternoon went to the depot where debris of crashed aircraft was on display. There was a lot of it and I did not know what I was looking for. I was given a cardboard box and adopting a knowledgeable and learned countenance, like that when at a buffet supper the canapes come round, I filled the box, which I entrusted to the RN aboard HMS *Bulldog* on my way back to Bayonne that night.

That afternoon I visited the family the Consul General had asked me to see. They lived in a charming country house, had not been molested in any way but for the present adopted a low profile. Back in Santander I was told that the airfield near by had been bombed that afternoon. I went there at once and sure enough the entire airfield was pockmarked with craters, which indicated medium size bombs dropped with precision by a formation of these bombers, probably HE 111s. There were no aircraft on the ground to be destroyed and no buildings either.

The following morning I went to our other British Embassy in Hendaye and was received by Sir Henry Chilton. He had been our Ambassador in Buenos Aires and knew some of my relations in the

56

Argentine so we had quite a chat. And so back to Valencia next day by train to Toulouse and on by air.

In Valencia, having written my reports and thank you letters, I started to plan a six week leave in UK. My secretary, Carmen, who lived in Valencia before the Civil War, told me that she knew several Spaniards who drove cars in the past, but had hidden them to avoid sequestration by the unions, while they themselves left the country or went into hiding or just kept a low profile. She had a friend who owned an almost new Morris 8 kept in hiding, and would sell it for £30 paid in sterling cash. I bought that car, put CD plates on it and drove it back to UK accompanied by Carmen who was also due for a holiday. It took five days in all, three on the road and two in Paris where the 1937 Exhibition was a pleasant contrast to our humdrum existence in Spain. When my six weeks' leave was up I returned to Valencia by the railway and aeroplane route. Carmen, whose holiday had been for four weeks only was already back and met me at the airport. She had a lot to tell.

While I had been away a row of fishermen's cottages on a sandy beach about fifteen miles south-west of Valencia had been taken over and refurbished to accommodate the Embassy staff. The officers' communications centre and chancery remained in Valencia and we had to commute each day between the town and the beach. The cottages were primitive, no baths or running water, and very poor lighting. In summer it was pleasant enough, as we spent a lot of time on the beach or in the sea, but if we were to spend a winter there it would be cold, isolated, and miserable.

The reason for this move, prompted by the Navy, was for our safety in the event of rioting or fighting on the streets of Valencia. The Navy would be expected to protect us and it would be simpler to do so if we were assembled on the beach than scattered round the town.

With regard to my job and the purpose of being there I felt frustrated. There was nothing I could report other than the information released to the press and my applications to see airfields, aircraft or front line action were always turned down, politely, with the very laudable explanation that if I were granted this privilege it must be open to the attachés of other countries, and many of them had their embassies full of potential enemies.

Then, towards the end of the year a letter arrived from DDAFL to say that I was to return to UK and would be attached to his staff pending a permanent posting. There would be no replacement to take over from me in Spain. There was no explanation and I wondered what I had done wrong. I suspected that the Ambassador must have requested my removal but why no replacement?

There seemed to be no urgency so I went down to El Grau, the port of Valencia, where usually there were three or four cargo ships flying the Red Duster. I found one bound for London, with a load of oranges, or was it tomatoes? and the Master agreed to take me. We would be at sea for six days including a few hours in Gibraltar. I have always enjoyed travelling in cargo ships and this was no exception.

Back in London I duly reported to DDAFL who was Group Captain, later Sir Victor Goddard or just V. G. He surprised me with the news that directly or through the Foreign Office he had been in touch with the Spanish Embassy in London and it had been agreed that an RAF mission should be invited to visit the territory under the control of the Government and would be permitted into the battlefield and have access to study the equipment in use by both sides. The mission was to consist of V.G. and myself.

In the interval between my leaving Valencia and returning to Spain, the Spanish Government had moved to Barcelona and our Embassy went there too, so when V.G. and I arrived at our destination it was Barcelona. We were met by Major Bayo who was to be our companion, adviser, guide and interpreter during the next two weeks. He took us to an hotel, where we were expected, and he would call back for us in an hour or so after a wash and a brush up, to go to the British Embassy. This was in a large house in a residential suburb of Barcelona (Calella). At the door we were told that His Excellency the Ambassador would receive V.G. I was shown into a very well furnished reception room with nobody there except Carmen. She explained that our other friends had decided to leave us alone together. It seemed astonishing to me that the Military Attaché, Major Richards, who was always referred to as 'The General', should not have been at the meeting between V.G. and the Ambassador. Perhaps he was but I was quite happy in Carmen's company.

Next morning we went to the office of my old acquaintance Colonel Camacho, who outlined our itinerary and V.G. gave his approval, and from there we took the road to Valencia. Our next destination was Madrid but the direct route was mostly in Franco's hands. The drive from Barcelona to Valencia was long enough but next day we set forth on, to me, a very familiar journey, from Valencia to Madrid. I do not remember where it was but we took a side road and arrived at an airfield where a lot of flying was in progress. It was a conversion unit where pilots who were already qualified to fly aged biplanes were now learning to fly Russian Mosca monoplanes. V.G. and I agreed that this was proof that we were trusted and welcome visitors. In Madrid our rooms were reserved in the Plaza Hotel, and we were glad to get to bed after so much driving.

Next day we visited the control and reporting centre. It was all that was needed or could be expected in the circumstances. The bombers would take off from the Nationalist airfield at Quatro Vientos, about twenty miles away to the south-west. They would be spotted by sympathizers or military outposts or perhaps by interception from wireless messages and reported to the control centre from whence an appropriate number of Moscas from Alcala de Henares, which lay about twenty-five miles east would be scrambled. The bombers would not venture over Madrid if the Moscas were there first. There had not been an effective raid for several weeks.

Then Major Bayo told us we would go to Guadalajara, the scene of victory over the Italian Fascists column. We drove out from Madrid on the Saragossa road, past Alcala de Henares and stopped just short of the town. This was the front, and to go any further would be dangerous. There were trenches and bunkers but not many soldiers to be seen. It was bitterly cold and I suppose only sentries were manning the trenches and the others were trying to keep warm elsewhere. We were reminded that the air attack on the Italian column took place while the column was in its own territory and before it reached no man's land which lay just ahead of where we were.

There were several light tanks or Bren-carriers close to where we stopped. They looked very similar to those used by the British Army (Cardon Lloyd I think they were called), so I took a peep inside. The instructions, notices and numerals were all in Russian so they may have been made under licence or copied.

Our next point of contact was to be the battle zone near Teruel and in the evening we were approaching a town on the way where we were to spend the night. V.G. was the epitome of an English gentleman. Tall and slim, well groomed and well dressed, he spoke in a quiet but authoritative tone with a trace of shyness. Major Bayo, our guide and contact was uncouth and garrulous and must have learned English in the Bronx of New York or perhaps in Puerto Rico, but he had a kindly disposition. The conversation went something like this. Bayo began, "Mee Colonel, now we come to Cuenca where we stay one night. I know Cuenca very well, many nice girls in Cuenca, I bring you a nice girl."

V.G. replied, "No thank you Major Bayo, don't bother. We have had a very long day."

Then Bayo, "Mee Colonel, you no like zee nice girls no?"

V.G. replied, "Look Major Bayo, I have been married for five years, I have two children and a happy and contented home."

But Major Bayo would not give up. "Mee Colonel," he said, "after you be married for five years you stroke zee bottom of your wife and it be the same you stroke the bottom of the Sargeant of Carabineros!"

I was sitting there listening to this unenlightened conversation and did not know whether to laugh or cry. I felt very very sorry for V.G. who was looking out of the window with a benign smile on his face and so we entered Cuenca in silence.

When we reached the battle zone next morning we were taken to an artillery battery, dug into the slope of a hill overlooking the valley of Teruel. It was equipped with 25-pounder field guns. There was also an observation post from where we had a much better view of the valley. There seemed to be nothing much happening and obviously we did not intend to fix bayonets so we retreated to Valencia and Barcelona. We thought we had come to the end of our visits, and since there was no running water in our luxury hotel, the WC did not flush and the whole place ponged we were not sorry to be going. However Major Bayo told us that we were expected to stay on for another two days, and these turned out to be the most interesting and informative of our visit.

Just north of Barcelona there is an isolated mountain which can be seen from miles around. It is Montserrat, 4,000 feet high. Major Bayo explained that we were on the way to an airfield of particular importance, which lay on the other side of that mountain and was not on a main road.

On arrival we noticed that there were hangars and permanent buildings, so it is probable that the airfield was there before the war. About half a dozen twin-engined sleek looking Russian bombers were parked on the tarmac in front of one of the hangars. I had seen bombers of the type in the air but not on the ground and often wondered what they bombed and whence and where. We were driven to the end hangar, got out of the car and went in. Lo and behold there stood a Heinkel 111 and a ME 109, both nearly new, serviceable and ready to fly. We asked how come these prime products of the German aircraft industry were here and on show to us? We were told that, on separate occasions these aeroplanes having landed, were lost and found themselves in Government territory.

Again, as in Bilbao, I did not know what to look for. V.G. got down to measuring or estimating the various angles of fire which could be used by the guns in the upper and lower rear turrets. I managed to extract a few rounds of ammunition from the ME 109 guns and put them in my pocket.

Next morning we had an appointment with the Senior Government representative, as yet unknown. It was to be in the offices established in Barcelona where the Government moved from Valencia. I remember vaguely his name was Sr Prieto, and I have no doubt that he was speaking on behalf of the Government. There were several other officials present, and sentries were on duty outside the building and the conference room. Following an exchange of introductions, handshakes, etc., we sat down to business. There was no agenda, but a monologue was delivered by Sr Prieto, a perfect oration for our benefit. The essence of his speech was as follows:

"Point No. 1 — the Government elected to rule Spain was not a Communist one, but a Socialist one. The Communists and the trade unions had organized the 'Revolution Social' and were responsible for the atrocities which had been committed. Countries, particularly those in Europe which were expected to give support to the democratic government of Spain, had not done so because of the chaos and distress which the social revolution had caused. We have had a war within a war and now the Government is in control. You can witness this by observing the unions no longer have their road blocks and there are no longer any corpses on the streets or in the mortuaries.

"Point No. 2 — The Nationalists are getting weapons, trained men, machines and other support from Germany and Italy. We need support also and expect it from those nations like Great Britain who believe in democracy.

"Point No. 3 — There will be another great war in Europe soon. If you support us now (Spain will probably remain neutral) we will be able to offer you the use of strategic harbours, airfields and the goodwill of the people."

The reasoning contained in this statement seemed so naîve that I abbreviated my translation. V.G. noticed this and gave me a mild rebuke saying that I was to translate every word.

When Sr Prieto finished, I expected some sort of debate or that V.G. would ask for enlightenment on certain aspects, e.g. what he had meant by support, was it moral, material or intervention with ships, aircraft and men? He remained silent as he had no mandate to speak on a matter which was the responsibility of the Foreign Office. He was after all just a very intelligent and capable RAF officer. He thanked Sr Prieto for receiving us and assured him that his words and opinions would be passed on to the appropriate authorities in Whitehall.

We did not call at the Embassy again, but went straight back to London. I remained attached to DDAFL for a few weeks, while the report on our visit was being prepared and then in March 1938 I was posted to RAF Station Hornchurch to command No. 54 Fighter Squadron.

CHAPTER IX

The War By Day

There were three fighter squadrons based at Hornchurch all equipped with Gloster Gladiators and expecting to receive Spitfires as soon as variable pitch or constant speed propellers were available. The first Spitfires had fixed pitch propellers and needed very long runways to take off. At Hornchurch we could offer only 1,000 yards. Duxford could offer at least 1,500 yards but even there they only just made it.

I arrived in early March 1938 and realized how little I knew about Fighter Command. Hornchurch was a 'Sector' station which meant that we had an Operations Room from which we controlled, by Radio Telephone (RT) the squadrons based there, giving them and their secondary units, flights, sections, down to individual aircraft orders to take off and land, the course to fly and height, etc. and whether to engage a potential enemy or not.

The Ops Room had a large map of the sector area which included much of the two adjacent sectors. On this map the WAAF plotters placed counters showing the movement of all aircraft in the area. Control and reporting is common knowledge today but as a newcomer I was impressed by the smooth efficiency with which it was applied in the Ops Room at Hornchurch. It was before the time when selected middle-aged officers were trained and then established as full-time controllers so I knew that I must, together with the COs of 74 Squadron and 65 Squadron, take my part in the Ops Room activities and be a Sector Controller.

The special code which was used to communicate with the Controller and the pilots was never intended for security purposes, but to simplify the exchange of messages. Later on it became essential for communications with our friends and allies who had come to Britain to continue their fight against the Nazis: the Norwegians, the French, and above all the Poles, who could not speak a word of English but knew exactly what to do when they heard "Number 303 Squadron scramble, 50 Bandits, Angels, 18 approaching from the South East. Vector 120."

I was intrigued by plots of aircraft flying thirty or forty miles out to sea, from whence they came and what was their origin. They were referred to as RDF plots and it was indiscreet to make enquiries about their origin. Today radar is commonplace but in 1938 its existence and its potential were known to a selected few only, mostly scientists, and the base for their tests and calibrations was at Orfordness on the Essex coast, in the Hornchurch Sector. Many of the interception practices which we did were probably used to calibrate the instruments at Orfordness. The senior boffin (this is an affectionate name for a scientist who worked on projects for the RAF) was Sir Robert Watson Watt.

The three Hornchurch Squadrons received their Spitfires in March 1939 and we took little time to adapt to the great change in performance, particularly the time to climb to 30,000 feet. These Spitfires had variable pitch propellers which made take off from Hornchurch no problem and also reduced the time to climb to 30,000 feet by several minutes. Later Spitfires were fitted with constant speed propellers which improved their all round performance even more.

At Hornchurch we carried on knowing that a war was most probable but taking minimum qualifying precautions.

September 3rd 1939 came and went but from then onwards a more serious mood prevailed. Our Spitfires had to be dispersed along the perimeter of the airfield, and the Army sent a detachment of soldiers to build bunkers with sandbags to protect them, and also to dig slit trenches where ground crews could shelter when bombs began to fall. There were new faces and new units to be seen almost everywhere.

I had been married for three months, and my wife and I occupied a house in the village of Hornchurch which was an official married quarter. Nevertheless this district would be in the front line as the war developed. Also 54 Squadron would probably be moved elsewhere or I might be posted to another unit. This was a problem that many families had to face but in our case the solution was a simple one. My father-in-law had bought a house in Oxfordshire and my wife could live there for the duration and join me when possible. We abandoned our married quarter and my wife went to her father's house in Whitchurch (Oxon). No. 54 Squadron had to move also, to Rochford (Southend).

Rochford airfield belonged to the Southend Municipal Authority and although we had visited there and made a provisional plan for its use as a satellite for the Hornchurch Sector, it was not until we were at war that it could be requisitioned. No. 54 Squadron was the first to move in, and we understood there would be problems: we would rotate with No. 65 and No. 74 in operating from Rochford. The first problem was accommodation. There were several wooden buildings and our plans included the use of these, but we were very overcrowded and looked forward to some expansion.

Early one morning soon after we arrived, I heard hammering going on in the adjacent building and I went out to investigate. I found two carpenters taking one of the wooden buildings to pieces and they explained that their bosses had a contract to take down all the buildings and reconstruct them at some future date. My problem was to stop them before we were sleeping out in the cold. The police agreed to help prevent the contractors from coming in and the sentry at the gate also had his orders. In the meantime we tried to discover who was responsible for this contract and how the situation could be remedied. It took a week to run to ground the right office in the Southend Municipal Authority.

When we had done our time at Rochford we returned to Hornchurch, and one day my younger brother, Max, appeared in my office to tell me that he was posted to No. 54 Squadron. He had been on a language course in France when war was declared but his base was a Hurricane squadron in Egypt. To return to Cairo in prevailing circumstances would serve no useful purpose and take a long time, so he went to London, reported to the Air Ministry, and was posted to Fighter Command and eventually to my squadron. I was not at all pleased about this because it would be difficult not to show him favours and also because both my Flight Commanders were junior to him and I had no intention of replacing them. I did not want to be accused of nepotism. It may be that I was rather harsh to Max, but he should never have been posted to my squadron. I did discuss this with the Station Commander but although sympathetic he could not get any support from headquarters.

Max got on well with the other officers and after I had left Hornchurch he took an active part in the air battles over Dunkirk. He was credited with shooting down four enemy aircraft but he did not return from his final sortie and was posted missing, presumed dead. Later, I made enquiries about him but no more was learned of his fate.

The squadron was back at Rochford during the cold spell of the winter 1939-40. The sea along the coast was frozen over and big ice patches lay on the airfield which had grass runways only.

This became a serious problem for our Spitfires because on landing the wheels would break up the ice and send it hurtling back against the flaps. We had changed several sets and then accepted the fact that we were grounded while the ice problem persisted but we still retained a section at readiness in case of an emergency.

It was late afternoon; Wonkey Way and Georgie Gribble were on patrol with me when the Controller told us that a bandit (i.e. enemy aircraft) was in our vicinity. This led to my one and only encounter in the air. Never before nor since were my guns fired in anger.

Under direction by RT from the Controller, we climbed to 12,000 feet and made several changes of course until Wonkey cried "Tally ho! Three o'clock." I turned in that direction and saw an HE 111 about 1,000 yards away, and decided to attack immediately to take the crew by surprise. I opened fire at about 200 yards and saw my tracer bullets peppering the target. A few tracers from the rear guns came my way but inspection on the ground confirmed that there were no hits on my Spitfire.

Fighter Command tactics at that time dictated that once the target was in range and gun sight lined up, the pilot should keep the guns firing until the ammunition was exhausted. The eight Browning machine-guns in each Spitfire (and Hurricane) were all activated together. In other words the pilot fired all eight together or none at all. I had expected to see some immediate effect from my onslaught so throttled back to watch Wonkey go in next, but just then the Heinkel dived almost vertically closely followed by Wonkey and Georgie. This dive was a tactic which we knew the Luftwaffe had adopted and practised and was most effective when there was cloud cover below to dive into. I was well above the cloud and asked the Controller for a course to steer for base. We were then at Rochford and before I landed I heard both Wonkey and Georgie requesting and receiving homing bearings also.

The Intelligence Officer supervised the debriefing and I learned that both my wing men had used all their ammunition before or after the target went into the cloud, which was very thin, and they saw the Heinkel with one undercarriage leg down looking "proper poorly". A week later wreckage of a Heinkel 111 was washed up on the Essex coast. We were credited with an enemy aircraft destroyed. This meant nothing to me.

In retrospect I now think I was wrong to go into the attack and I would have had a hero's welcome if I had led that aeroplane and crew back to Rochford. This should have been possible with Georgie and Wonkey and sixteen Browning guns bringing up the rear and my leading the way and making sure that the Heinkel crew knew that they were prisoners of war. I still believe that Luftwaffe airmen had mothers and sweethearts in spite of Hitler, and some had children too.

What did mean something to me was that our RDF and Control and Reporting Systems made the interception of an enemy aircraft about 20 miles out to sea and without any assistance from the ground. It may have been done before, but the date I have in mind is January 24th 1940. My Flying Log Book on that date records an operational patrol of one hour.

I had known the AOC No. 11 Group, Sir Keith Park before, when I was seconded to the Peruvian Air Force and he was the British Air Attaché South America, based in Buenos Aires but with a roving commission. I was on his visiting list. We met also on his frequent and friendly visits to squadrons in his Group. He told me that my two years as a Squadron CO were nearly up and he wanted me to join his staff as Wing Commander Training, but it would mean waiting a month or so until the present incumbent was posted and promoted. He was Harry Broadhurst, later Sir Harry, so I returned to Rochford with my squadron for the third time.

There was a row of holiday bungalows along the fence of the airfield which were empty. I discovered the name and address of the owner of one of them and he agreed to rent it to me so that I could use it for my accommodation and also bring my wife Jane to stay there while No. 54 Squadron was at Rochford. A field telephone was installed between the bungalow and the premises used as the Officers' Mess and also to Flying Control and so we moved in.

One morning I returned from patrol and at the entrance to the Mess was met by the Squadron Intelligence Officer who was very excited indeed. A spy had been caught; a lady taking photographs of our Spitfires through the fencing of the airfield. Just then the field telephone rang and a frightened voice told me that the bungalow was surrounded by police who had confiscated her camera and were asking a lot of questions about her past and in particular why she was at Southend.

At last the police were persuaded that she was taking very innocent photographs and that she was the CO's wife.

At the end of March we returned to Hornchurch and my posting to HQ No. 11 Group as Wing Commander Training was confirmed. Also my successor as CO 54 Squadron was nominated. Although D.J. was a very worthy and popular man he had spent no time in Fighter Command and when the Nazis invaded the Netherlands in May it was evident that he must give way to someone with more experience. The choice fell on Flight Lieut. J. A. Leathart, known as 'Prof' on account of his professional qualifications.

'Prof' had joined the squadron as a Pilot Officer from the City of Chester 610 Auxiliary Squadron of which he was a founder member at the same time, given a week or two, as me. We were married within a fortnight of each other, we were on staff duties together and commanded night fighter squadrons and were in the same headquarters during the invasion. We retired before qualifying for full pension and went into business together, and now live within ten miles of each other.

The Ops Room at Uxbridge was underground. I don't know how many feet but one felt pretty safe down there. Harry Broadhurst had very kindly arranged for my wife and I to take over the rent of an attractive little bungalow, near Gerrards Cross, where he had lived and I was ready to become a staff officer although I had not been to Staff College.

I was to work in an office in the Headquarters buildings above ground and was expected to make sure that the pilots of all the squadrons in the Group completed their training syllabus, to visit the squadrons, listen to their suggestions, and assess their capabilities. I was also to be a Controller in the Ops Room.

In my office there was a small table and chair, occupied from time to time by either HRH Prince George Duke of Kent or Lord Clydesdale. HRH was very seldom there and I did not ask what he was reading but supposed it was Intelligence reports. Lord Clydesdale had the task of studying accident reports and deciding who or what was to blame. After the Rudolph Hess affair he abandoned his chair in the corner and went north. I genuinely missed him because he had such a warm and sincere personality, I could hardly believe that he was the first to fly over Mount Everest, that he was Amateur Boxing Champion of Britain and that he was the Heir Apparent to the Premier Dukedom of Scotland.

The Ops Room at Uxbridge was by far the most active and informative of them all, because displayed here were not only the plotted tracks of enemy raids and often there were several of these coming in at the same time, but also a vertical panel at the back showing the state of readiness of our fighter squadrons, arranged under the sector stations on which they were based. Thus, under Hornchurch would be three squadrons and if one was at Standby it would be yellow another at Readiness in red and the third one Released in green. There were some small compartments, each with a telephone, on both sides of the room, for communication with other services such as the AA guns, the Balloons and Air Raid warnings. But the Controller was fully occupied in trying to ensure that every incoming raid was intercepted, even by an inadequate number of our fighters, before it reached the target which was assumed to be one or other of 11 Group's airfields. Once intercepted these Luftwaffe formations broke up and seldom dropped their bombs accurately.

The Group Controller would instruct the Sector Controller as follows: "Hornchurch Sector engage bandits 170 with one flight." The plots for raid 170 would be tagged and the change in readiness recorded on the panel.

The blitzkrieg began on May 10th 1940 with the invasion of Holland by an unprecedented force of paratroops and ten Panzer divisions of tanks. Against this formidable array of military might Fighter Command sent ten Blenheims of No. 600 Squadron to protect the city of Rotterdam. No doubt this token force was intended to assure the people of Holland that we would protect them and was ordered at the highest level but only two Blenheims returned. No. 600 Squadron had lost more than half its aircrews, and these could not be replaced quickly because it was the City of London Auxiliary Squadron. The aircraft did not matter because they were obsolescent and due to be replaced by Beaufighters. I doubt whether the good citizens of Rotterdam were ever aware of this sacrifice, they had far bigger problems to live with. No. 600 Squadron was I suppose the first unit of Fighter Command committed to oppose the blitzkrieg.

The German Wehrmacht and Luftwaffe continued their relentless, well planned, timed and orchestrated advance through Holland, Belgium and into France. It was here in France that the Advanced Air Striking Force was based. It contained several Hurricane Squadrons which had previously been in Fighter Command, and one of these was No. 501 City of Bristol Auxiliary Squadron, commanded by Squadron Leader M. V. Clube (See Chapter VII). His experiences were more fortunate than most. When communications with headquarters were severed, when refugees began to jam the roads and when it was apparent that his squadron must either be exterminated or get out, he chose the latter. The Hurricanes were flown to Jersey and the vehicles, ground crews and other members of the squadron made a three day journey by road and sea to get there too. They found a cross Channel ferry boat to take them to Portland.

Not one aeroplane or vehicle or airman was lost when the squadron assembled at Tangmere. That evening No. 501 Squadron was called to Night Readiness but my friend 'Club' explained that none of his auxiliary pilots had flown by night before and they had just been through an exhausting experience, so they were 'released'.

For a few days there was chaos at airfields near the coast such as Tangmere. There were single pilots and groups of two or three flying in from France, glad to be back in UK but very demoralized. There were others with orders to fly to France as reinforcements for units, supposedly in action there but no doubt already overrun by the Germans. At 11 Group Headquarters we did our best to clear the decks for action in the immediate future. Squadrons were reconstructed where possible at their former bases. Odd aeroplanes, pilots and ground crews were posted to other units to make up their strength. The situation at Dunkirk was not unforeseen and preparations were being made for it.

No training could be done by squadrons in No. 11 Group and we had to rely on the other Groups, outside the combat zone, to provide trained replacements. Thus I spent part of each day, or night, below ground in the Ops Room and part of it in my office at ground level. I took advantage of the light aeroplanes provided by our Communications Flight at Northolt to visit squadrons and try to help solve their problems.

As expected Fighter Command and in particular No. 11 Group, were called upon to prevent the Luftwaffe from dominating the skies over the beaches of Dunkirk. This time, unlike the Hurricanes which had been based in France and lost contact with their headquarters, these would operate from the UK under the direct control of their own Ops Room. For the first time Spitfires were allowed to fly over the Continent. Even so the men on the beaches were disheartened when they saw so few of our fighters overhead. They failed to understand that the time to intercept bombers is before they reach their target and release their bombs — not after.

When Dunkirk was over there was little activity for a few weeks while the Luftwaffe consolidated its forces on the Continent for the next round, which turned out to be attacks on shipping, particularly convoys in the English Channel and North Sea. The bombers were escorted mainly by ME 110s, two seater twin engine fighters, and in spite of their high performance these aeroplanes proved to be vulnerable in combat to our Spitfires and Hurricanes more so than the ME 109. This was probably because of their manoeuvrability or lack of it. These attacks on shipping lanes were a useful contribution to our experience and knowledge. At Dunkirk squadrons were sent to reconnoitre and seek action but the defence of our convoys was conducted within RDF (radar) and RT range of our Control and Reporting systems and units were 'scrambled' only when they were needed. Many ships were lost but the convoys around our coasts continued throughout the war.

And so we, that is the reader and I, come to the Battle of Britain. So much has been written about it with documentary authentification that I will not venture to step in where Angels fear to tread. There is however one episode which will always remain on my mind. The personal animosity between the AOC No. 11 Group Sir Keith Park and the AOC No. 12 Group Sir Trafford Leigh Mallory.

I was on the staff of Sir Keith since I left Hornchurch in March 1940 and first met him in South America when he visited Peru. I was on the staff of Sir Trafford when he took over as AOC No. 11 Group, after the Battle of Britain, but when the night bombing of our cities, both coastal and inland, was beginning I was also on the staff of Sir Trafford when he was C.-in-C. Fighter Command in 1943. Briefly the argument was this. Sir Trafford inferred that Sir Keith was conducting the battle without the final object in view, namely the destruction of the enemy in the air. He advocated large formations of fighters which would outnumber the enemy and sweep clean the skies of south-east England once or twice a day. Sir Keith responded that his airfields, radar masts, runways, Ops Room, etc. must be defended otherwise the whole of our air defence in the south-east would crumble. No airfield or other installations in 12 Group had been attacked nor were likely to be whereas many in 11 Group had and would continue to suffer. Both AOCs were right but the circumstances were entirely different in each Group. The pilots much preferred being in 12 Group where they enjoyed a less hazardous and less arduous existence and could win a lot more medals.

Finally both were directed by the C.-in-C. to pursue the strategy which each advocated within his own Group, and this was done. It is, however, sad to record that two such gifted and distinguished Commanders should have engaged in a personal vendetta at such a critical time.

RAF College, Cranwell

Avro Tutors flying over Cranwell, 1931

Brother Max (far right) Flight Cadet, Cranwell

HMP with his rebuilt Austin Whippet — 1929

Prototype of Austin Whippet

The author with Freddie West (far right) in Malta

Mount Etna

Christmas Day 1930, Malta — senior NCOs visit officers of 202 Squadron

Fairey IIIF seaplane — Malta 1930

Fairey IIID float plane, 202 Squadron

No. 202 Squadron moored on the Nile — 1931

Supermarine Southampton

Supermarine S6 — Schneider Cup winner

Author flying in formation over Malta in Fairey IIID

No. 202 Squadron ready to depart on a cruise to Khartoum (HMP first left front row)

Form 985.

ROYAL AIR FORCE.

CERTIFICATE.

THIS IS TO CERTIFY that   Flying Officer H. McD. Pearson.

has completed XXXXXXXXXXXXXXXXXXXX   The 39th Flying Instructors'
Course.

at The Central Flying School.

The duration of the course was from   20.9.32   to   17.12.32.

He has passed, obtaining 82 % of the total Marks.

Remarks (if any) by Officer Commanding unit at which the course was held :—

Outstandingly suitable for employment as an instructor.
An excellent all round officer. Average in technical subjects.
Recommended for "A"2 Category. Qualified to instruct in
instrument flying.

Signed................................ Group Captain.
Officer Commanding.
C.F.S., Wittering.

Dated...... 21.12.32.

Certificate — Flying Instructor

3 Instructors at Las Palmas — Capt. Luigi Bianci (Instructor on fighters, Royal Italian Air Force), Capt. Cesar Alvares (Instructor on flying, Peruvian Air Force), and the author (Captain and Instructor in bombing and armament)

Bomber and armament cadets with Commander Washburn of the CAP with the author

Group Capt. Keith Park, Air Attaché South America (later the famous AOC 11 Group, Sir Keith) visits the Cadet College at Las Palmas

Peruvian, Brazilian and Columbian delegates discussing the frontier problem at Laticia

River steamer on the Ucayali

Curtiss fighter on floats

Royal Navy visit to Lima

HMP's marriage to Jane, 13th May 1939

Our idyllic house in Cornwall, 1942

HMP with Jane — Lima, 1947

HM Queen Mary visits Charmy Down

*Brother Alec and friend, and
(below) Alec (3rd from left)
somewhere in India*

'The Pup' takes to the road with daughter Frances at the wheel, and below, with Simoncito as co-driver

H. E. the British Ambassador welcomes Peruvian team back from the 1948 Olympics where they won gold for shooting. Author is on duty.

Civil aviation conference in Lima, 1948

DDAFL (the author) conducts Air Attachés to observe the Berlin airlift

The author — 'intrepid aviator'

The author — CO at Kai-Tak

Staff officers at Fontainbleau

The author with General Norstadt, Supreme Commander, NATO

CHAPTER X

The War By Night

In late 1940 when winter approached, we in Fighter Command, and
in particular No. 11 Group, appraised the situation. We had won the
first round and proved that bombers with no fighter escort could not
penetrate to their inland targets without suffering unacceptable losses.
Also that fighters had a limited radius of action which must apply to the
bombers too. However, this was the case by day only, not by night, and
so we must examine the problem from a very different aspect. Suppose
the bombers flew by night, then every large city, its population and its
factories would be vulnerable, and all within range. Our Spitfires and
Hurricanes would be worse than useless unless searchlights could
illuminate and hold a target, which they could not do, even on clear
nights. The AA guns made a lot of noise which was encouraging to the
average citizen, but who could assess their efficiency as with the
searchlights? It would not be very popular with pilots of Spitfires and
Hurricanes to be sent to patrol London East at 20,000 feet to see if our
guns could bring them down. Also an enormous investment in men
and material would be needed to give just the token AA defence to each
and all of our centres of population.

Sir Keith left No. 11 Group for a senior appointment in the Far East
and Sir Trafford became AOC No. 11 Group. He lost no time in
organizing his squadrons into wing formations and his wing formations
into a Group Formation. However, these formations had little purpose
to fulfil. They flew over the Pas de Calais and Picardy challenging the
Luftwaffe to battle. At first there was a mild reaction but very soon the
Luftwaffe decided to stay on the ground, well protected from low flying
attack by their truly lethal light AA Batteries and knowing that no target
of importance existed within the range of No. 11 Group fighters.

Air Commodore 'Gobbo' Gibbs, later to become Sir Gerald, had
been Senior Air Staff Officer (SASO) to Sir Keith Park during the
Battle of Britain and continued in that capacity for a month or more to
ensure continuity. He summoned me to his office to discuss my future.
The AOC he said would invite me to be one of his Wing Leaders but

wanted to be sure that I would welcome this compliment before he interviewed me himself. I replied that I had become interested in the Night Air Defence problem and would much prefer to be chosen as CO of a Night Fighter Squadron. Would he please thank the AOC for his kind offer which I did appreciate most sincerely.

Gibbs then suggested that I should dedicate as much time as I could spare, bearing in mind that I was still on the roster in the Ops Room as a Group Controller, to find out what had been done and was being done and what should be done to prevent the total destruction of our cities.

I started with visits to Headquarters Fighter Command at Bentley Priory and in particular to the signals branch which included both radio and radar (RT and RDF in those days). A great deal had been done and the boffins were testing prototypes, at the FIU (Fighter Interception Unit) at Ford in South Sussex, of the equipment which would be at our disposal to intercept and destroy enemy bombers in darkness. The basic requirements and the state of the art of night flying were as follows:

(i) The Sector Controller would see from plots on his board, that a raid was heading towards his territory. He would scramble one or two night fighters and direct them to a well-known orbit area not visible in darkness, but adjacent.

(ii) He would hand over one of the fighters in orbit to the control of the GCI (Ground Control Interception) Unit. These units carried extremely accurate radar with a range of about fifty miles radius. The Controller had his own RT frequency so could concentrate on his task which was to put his night fighter in AI contact with the target. They were the first to use the presentation of radar echoes on the cathode ray tube in such a form that the Controller could conduct an interception by looking at the tube only and not at plots. It was known as the Plan Position Indicator (PPI) tube and has been developed since to serve many ramifications of radar, primarily in ships, large and small.

(iii) Three types of AI (Air Interception) radar came into service in Fighter Command during the war. The first was A Mark IV in Beaufighters and it was with this combination that early successes were achieved. Nevertheless its range was limited to the height of the aeroplane above the ground or sea. Also accuracy depended on the adjustment and calibration of external aerials mounted on the airframe whereas the later ones used a much higher frequency and a small aerial in the centre of a reflector disc in the nose of the aeroplane. They needed no calibration nor adjustment and were effective low down. These were the Mark VIII and Mark X both mounted in Mosquito night fighters. In the former the reflector disc and aerial rotated spinally and in the latter they moved horizontally.

The one Sector Ops Room where I might see theory become practice was at Kenley, near to Redhill where No. 600 Sqdn. was receiving its first Beaufighters with Mark IV AI; close to Ford where the FIU boffins were testing and assessing their new inventions and not very far from Uxbridge where I was based.

I went to Kenley on several occasions and looked in at Redhill on the way there or back. Twice I found the C.-in-C. sitting alone in the Ops Room asking for clarification on the technicalities of the equipment being used and the presentation of the radar. It was he who sponsored, approved and ordered these advanced items of equipment just as he had done with the Hurricanes and Spitfires, and no doubt he was anxious to witness their progress. I wondered whether he visited No. 600 Squadron at Redhill because a lot had to be done there before this equipment could get a fair trial in an operational squadron.

Redhill had a grass surface with a runway length of about 1,000 yards. An average pilot would be wary landing there by day in a Beaufighter; moreover flying was still restricted because, although the massive raids by the Luftwaffe were over, there were still small forays into 11 Group territory where there was an unwritten rule that all twin-engined aircraft were hostile. To get to more appropriate areas in which to fly unhindered, such as 10 Group or 12 Group territory the Ops Room was expected to inform everyone concerned, the AA gunners, the Observer Corps, the Balloon Control, etc. To give pilots opportunity to get to know their new aircraft by day and by night arrangements were made for a small number to fly from Debden and Tangmere and do their training away from sensitive 11 Group territory.

There was the problem of the selection and training of AI Radar Operators. No provision had been made for these unknown animals and the Officer in Charge of Records naturally assumed they had a pretty low IQ. One particular example was an airman, posted to 600 Sqdn. as an AI Operator who came from a rustic locality. On reporting he saw a strange object on the desk and is reported to have said, "What manner of thing be that? It be a telephone I hear tell."

One day in my office I took a telephone call from Air Commodore Orlebar inviting me to lunch at the RAF Club. He had commanded the High Speed Flight when I was at Calshot in 1929. We arranged a date and time but I did not ask the purpose of our meeting. There were just the two of us having a tête-à-tête lunch together.

He told me that the Vice Chief of Air Staff at the Air Ministry, Sir Sholto Douglas, later Lord Douglas, had been appointed to succeed Sir Hugh Dowding, and was very soon to become Commander-in-Chief of Fighter Command. He had made Night Air Defence his first priority and was already planning and selecting staff for a new branch at Bentley Priory, which would keep in touch with all the ramifications of this subject and advise and report to him.

Orlebar went on to say that there would be some ten to fifteen staff officers in this new branch and would I like to be one of them? I accepted without hesitation. Sir Sholto joined us for coffee. Needless to say Orlebar had been appointed Officer in Charge of the New Branch Ops 3. I already knew most of those who had been selected and at Bentley Priory Ops 1 was dedicated to War by Day, Ops 2 to control and reporting and Ops 3 War by Night. All three branches were accommodated in offices close to one another. Each had an immediate boss but took a lead from the SASO (Senior Air Staff Officer) whose office was next door to the C.-in-C. He was Air Vice-Marshal Callaway, known as 'Cab'. It was to him that the Branch Leaders went to present their individual problems and we of the Ops 3 Branch had a very good spokesman in Orlebar.

The first and major task, to which we were committed, was to prepare a blueprint plan for the Night Air Defence which could be implemented by existing or soon-to-come advanced equipment and with the bulldozers, chartered surveyors, and local solicitors who were essential for the infrastructure of new sites.

It takes longer to train an operational aircrew than to build a night fighter aeroplane. The first priority was to get a night fighter OTU (Operational Training Unit) off the ground. Its purpose was to introduce young recently qualified pilots to equally young, but academically qualified AI Radar Operators, and both to the Beaufighter and AI Mark IV.

They would have to spend many hours flying by instruments by night and last but not least, learn to creep up on one another with the help of GCI and AI radar until a dark shape could be seen ahead and very close.

Church Fenton in Yorkshire was chosen for the OTU because it was in existence and met our requirements for runways, lighting and accommodation. We were fortunate that Group Captain R. L. Atcherley (Batchy) was appointed Commanding Officer of the Station and Commandant of the OTU. He later became Sir Richard.

We estimated that about 20 squadrons would be needed and the use of a corresponding number of approved airfields and GCI Units. These units were mobile, whereas the airfields were not.

Although the build up of aircraft equipment and infrastructure went ahead with all speed, it was not a happy time for Ops 3. One of our staff went on duty in the Ops Room every night and wrote a short report before coming off next morning. These reports had a monotonous trend as one after another of our great cities was bombed with superb accuracy by the Luftwaffe and we had not destroyed a single one of their bombers. When coming off duty we felt somewhat ashamed at our failure, and no one more so than Air Commodore Orlebar. He was not on any roster but would be in the Ops Room from after dark when the first RDF plots appeared until the board was cleared, then he would go to our office and write notes and instructions to be implemented next day. We were so attached and loyal to him that we were anxious about his health and knew that he must sleep and not worry all night and every night. We wanted him to be his normal and responsible self. Group Captain Harcourt Smith (Smidge) who like myself had been recruited from No. 11 Group HQ was a man endowed with great charm and tact, and was Orlebar's deputy; so one morning we all happened to be in the ante-room of the Officers' Mess at Bentley Priory at lunch-time. Smidge came in with Orlebar and guided the conversation towards the effect lack of sleep was having on the rest of his staff. They continued a constructive and friendly conversation, the result being that Smidge would take the keys of Orlebar's office and filing cabinet every evening and then go home with them. He lived twelve miles away. Orlebar agreed to allow this to be done for a limited time only. It was a great success and it made our office work and our nightly vigils much easier.

In August 1941 there was a change of heart in Ops 3. Our night fighters were beginning to have limited success and although they never achieved the critical ten per cent attrition rate on the German bombers it did show that we were on the right track. Credit for this must be given to No. 604 Squadron and the FIU.

No. 604 (County of Middlesex) was one of the three Auxiliary Squadrons based on Hendon but never suffered the losses which were inflicted on No. 600 Squadron. Nor had it been called upon to fly Beaufighters with radar from an inadequate airfield like Redhill. In fact 604 Squadron had everything in its favour and made the most of it. It was in no way demoralized so wanted to get going.

The squadron was based at Middle Wallop on Salisbury Plain being a sector station in No. 10 Group with its own Ops Room there. The airfield was and still is a grass one with no hard runway, but the approaches, airfield lighting, accommodation, etc. were all well within the perimeter set by Ops 3, and the Sector GCI Unit was at Sopley — not far away. Its greatest asset was the talent available from officers and airmen within the squadron. There was a surplus of qualified pilots who saw the problem and accepted the challenge.

Consider first the Squadron Commander, John Cunningham, who in civil life was a test pilot for de Havilland. He was a perfectionist and with his AI Operator, Jimmy Rawnsley, worked in such perfect harmony that they seldom missed an opportunity to bring an AI contact to a successful conclusion. They were credited with the destruction of more enemy aircraft than any other night fighter crew. John Cunningham became CO of 604 Squadron, and after serving as a Staff Officer at HQ 11 Group, he was appointed to command 85 Squadron at Swannington, Norfolk, where the Squadron became part of No. 100 Group under the operational arm of Bomber Command.

Consider next that argumentative extrovert Derek Jackson who, in the squadron records, was an 'Officer Air Gunner'. He was in fact an Oxford Don and knew as much or more about radar and radio than the boffins on whom we depended for advice and education. What is more he took to the air and inspired enthusiasm by his skill, knowledge and success. In a Beaufighter there was plenty of room in the back for a third person to benefit from instruction and demonstration so that Jackson together with Rawnsley, took upon themselves the task of training the surplus aircrews to become AI Operators as well as Pilots.

Another member of 604 Squadron remembered for his personality and achievements is Rory Chisholm, who before the war was a brilliant junior executive in an international oil company. He was very successful also in the art of converting an AI contact into a bull's-eye on the target. He was appointed Commanding Officer of the FIU where he continued to fly on night operations. Some time later he was appointed SASO to the AOC No. 100 Group in Bomber Command.

And then there was Chris Hartley, who came to 604 Squadron from Eton where he was a schoolmaster. He went on to become CO of the FIU and decided to stay on in the Royal Air Force after the war. He was granted a permanent commission, attained the rank of Air Marshal and was knighted.

Although heartened by these early successes there was a long way to go before we could stop the nightly Luftwaffe attacks. More squadrons had to be formed, more aircrew trained, more ground and air radar supplied and a lot more experience gained. Nevertheless one morning Wing Commander Pretty (later Sir Walter) the Chief Signals Officer at Bentley Priory and a contemporary of mine at Cranwell, suggested to me in confidence that I should be in the Ops Room that evening and I was there. We knew that the target was Birmingham and shortly after dusk the plots began to appear across the Channel and North Sea, heading in that direction with the usual precision. Then as they approached the target they began to scatter and go in all directions and no bombs fell on Birmingham that night.

We in Ops 3 were aware that KG 100, the Pathfinders of the Luftwaffe were guided to their target by a very narrow high frequency radio beam and the problem was to detect the frequency, a task which seemed almost impossible by conventional methods. Then a Heinkel 111 of KG 100 came to rest in Britain with its black boxes intact so it became possible to disrupt the navigational process on which the German bombers were entirely dependent. The application of this knowledge was to deceive the visiting team. It probably took many forms but it became known as 'Bending the Beam'.

None of us in Ops 3 thought for a moment that it was the end of the purpose for which we had been conceived at such a high level. We expected that KG 100 and the main force of bomb carriers would be back again with a new box of tricks at their disposal, but it never happened, so full marks to our Signals Branch and the boffins who worked with them. Hitler took his main bomber force to Russia and we in Ops 3 had a well trained and housed and expanding night fighter force and no bandits to engage. It is true that a small number of German bombers was left in France and the Netherlands and on occasions these would attack undefended towns such as Bath and Cambridge and also ports and harbours on our coasts, but they did not penetrate into the industrial heartland as before and were never again a nightly event.

In August 1941 Orlebar was promoted to Air Vice-Marshal and appointed AOC No. 10 Group with his headquarters at Rudloe in Wiltshire. His successor as head of Ops 3 was Air Commodore Elliot (later Sir William) a most appropriate choice because he was previously the Station CO at Middle Wallop where No. 604 Squadron was based. In mid-September the AOC 10 Group (Orlebar) telephoned to remind me of his undertaking to offer me command of a night fighter squadron when a vacancy arose and suggested No. 600 Squadron which I accepted gratefully. It was based for the time being at Colerne.

The squadron had moved from Redhill to Catterick in Yorkshire where it was reconstituted. Few if any of the Auxiliary personnel remained and it was equipped with Beaufighter II aircraft. It was destined for Predannack, a new airfield built on moorland and bog a few miles from The Lizard in Cornwall. The reason for this remote location was that the air raids on Merseyside cities, Clydeside cities and also Belfast had used the Irish Sea and St George's Channel as the approach route, probably helped to some extent by the lights of Dublin. By having a night fighter airfield and two GCI Units within control distance of this route we might well be able to exact a toll. Also some protection could be given in South-West Wales to such places as Port Talbot and Milford Haven.

We remained at Colerne about a month before moving from there to Predannack. On arrival we found many things for which we were grateful. The runways were long and broad, the lighting and flying control were up to standard. Our Sector Station Operations Room was competent and welcomed our arrival although it was thirty miles away.

The Sector Ops Room was at Portreath and the GCI Units one at Coverack and the other on St Mary's, Isles of Scilly. Liaison and personal contact between GCI Units and night fighter squadrons was always encouraged and indeed transport was provided for that purpose, but the only way to get to St Mary's was by borrowing the Magister which was allocated to the Station Commander and had a complement of two only. No wonder the liaison with Coverack was on a much firmer basis and contacts (not AI ones) were established each day, and probably by night also for those off duty. It was manned one hundred per cent by WAAFs, all top grade ones from top to bottom.

The accommodation was excellent because the hotels which once flourished on this coast had been closed and were at our disposal. The Polurian was requisitioned for the officers and the Poldhu and several smaller ones for the NCOs and airmen.

The Station Commander was Wing Commander M. V. Clube, my close friend from Filton days. We both held the same rank and that could have led to squabbles and intrigues in other circumstances but we knew each other so well that I saluted him when I entered his office and he saluted me when he entered mine and then we both sat down to discuss our problems together.

My problem was the Beaufighter II which was an unnecessary aeroplane and a dangerous one, and one that Ops 3 had never asked for.

It seems it was ordered because the Rolls-Royce Merlin engines which supplied its power gave more at height altitude than the Hercules for which the Beaufighter was designed. It was intended to counter a high level threat, which never materialized. The change of engines altered the centre of gravity and made the aircraft unstable on the ground at low speeds. This in turn gave it a tendency to swerve off to the right on take off and a coarse use of rudder was needed to keep straight. A much more serious defect was known as 'The Shimmy'. This was a violent vibration generating at the tail end of the aircraft after landing but extending to the whole fuselage.

Various remedies were suggested and tried without success. In the meantime the Squadron Engineer Officer Charles Goodacre made an internal inspection of all the tail plane structures and found components loose and bent. One aircraft failed to return from a patrol out at sea. The pilot had been in RT contact which ceased abruptly with no explanation.

All our Beaufighter IIs were grounded and we were told we would be re-equipped with Beaufighter VIs when these were available.

It was February 1942. We had been blessed with a mild winter in Cornwall and were still enjoying life there. My wife Jane and our little boy Bruce were with me and we rented a picturesque and cosy little cliff top house, overlooking a sandy beach and only ten minutes' walk from the Officers' Mess in the Polurian Hotel. Anne was there too, being both nanny and housemaid. Rationing was almost non-existent. We had enjoyed the last weeks of summer 1941 and hoped secretly that we would be grounded again in the summer of 1942. However that was not to be because Beaufighter VIs began to arrive, one by one, and I spent less time in those idyllic surroundings. I put myself on the roster again which meant sleeping at dispersal once or twice a week and flight testing my aeroplane in the afternoon, and on some nights a routine patrol.

The AOC No. 10 Group (Orlebar) telephoned to ask whether I would be prepared to become Station Commander of RAF Colerne. I was taken aback. Colerne was a vast Sector Station with two independent Maintenance Units (MUs) based there and four satellite airfields. Also there was a day fighter squadron (Whirlwinds) and a night fighter squadron (Beaufighter Is but converting to Mosquitoes) and one Turbinelite-cum-Hurricane squadron near by at Charmy Down.

Operational problems could be decentralized and resolved quickly but I suppose the reason for my appointment was my experience in such matters. Responsibility for administration was much more irksome. I estimated there would be under my wing some several thousand officers and airmen and probably 400 WAAFs. All of them expected housing, meals, promotion or punishment and I had no experience in these responsibilities except for the few months I spent at Filton in 1936 (see Chapter VII).

In due course I became grateful to the competent and loyal staff who brought to my attention only those problems they were not authorized to handle themselves. I was 34 years old at the time. I accepted, was promoted to Group Captain (Acting) and went to Colerne.

Jane, Bruce and Anne stayed on in Cornwall until the lease expired and then returned to Whitchurch. Colerne is a brick-built station planned before the war and only half finished in September 1939. Thereafter the construction of essential buildings was accelerated and non-essential ones ceased. Married quarters of all grades, including the CO's residence came into the latter category. This meant that my family could not live there with me, nor could other families.

On the evening of 26th April 1942 I was having a bath in the WAAF Officers' Mess. This was not a regular practice; indeed I had not done it before nor since, but the hot water system in the Officers' Mess was being serviced and I had accepted the privilege to bath and dine with the WAAF officers.

The telephone rang and I was put through to the Ops Room. About twenty bandits were plotted approaching Bath, which is very close to Colerne. They were flying low and were not on the radar screen until nearing the coast where the ROC (Royal Observer Corps) picked them up. Night fighters had been scrambled. There were no ground based defences around Bath. The air raid warnings had been alerted.

When I reached the Ops Room there was no doubt that Bath was the target.

All available Hurricanes from Charmy Down had been scrambled on orders from No. 10 Group and we had two or three Mosquitoes or Beaufighters on patrol. Middle Wallop had some also but it was not the numbers that mattered because the more we put into the air the greater the confusion. With AI Mark IV the distance at which a contact could be established and pursued was the same as the height of your aircraft above the ground. The raiders were flying at under 2,000 feet above sea level and Bath was surrounded by hills perhaps 500 feet high. I went from the Ops Room to the Flying Control tower and from there I could see the flashes of bombs exploding on the beautiful and unprotected City of Bath. I wondered whether the citizens had found shelter and how many had not. I felt humiliated that a small number of bandits was able to penetrate so far inland and get out again without loss. It was not only that I was the Commander of two airfields where so many day and night fighters were based, but also that I had been a member of Ops 3 at Bentley Priory.

In the early summer of 1942 my benefactor, the AOC No. 10 Group Air Vice-Marshal Orlebar died. He had been suffering from cancer for several months and it was with great sadness that I attended the funeral at his family home in Northamptonshire. His successor as AOC No. 10 Group was Air Vice-Marshal Steele (later to become Sir Charles) a man of great ability and intellect. I had met him before when he was SASO to the AOC No. 9 Group at Preston Lancs, and later I was privileged to serve on his staff in No. 85 Group as SASO.

The United States were at war from the day of Pearl Harbor, 7th December 1941. They were building up massive forces of men and quantities of material to operate on three fronts; Europe, North Africa and the Pacific. So far, in the summer of 1942, we at Colerne had seen in our two MUs a few US aircraft being converted to our needs and on our airfields a few lease-lend ones in operational units. We were yet to see the multitude of well-trained and equipped soldiers, sailors and airmen who were to arrive here in 1943, but we did have a glimpse of the shape of things to come.

I was told by 10 Group Headquarters that twelve USAAF (United States Army Air Force) officers would arrive at Colerne on a date specified. They would fly in direct from the US and leave two weeks later, the same way. They were coming to study our Ops Room and everything connected therewith. They must be accommodated in the Officers' Mess and live with us and share all our secrets. When they arrived and had settled in, we at Colerne were most favourably impressed by these young officers. They were well groomed, well dressed, intelligent and obviously anxious to learn all we had to teach. No doubt they were grateful too for our friendship and hospitality but they had not seen England yet nor that part of it where people lived in country houses.

I discussed this with Wing Commander Joe Offard, the Senior Administrative Officer and my adjutant Squadron Leader Acton. We agreed to select six or more country homes with gardens and ask the owner or occupant to give lunch to two American officers on the Sunday before they returned to America, and to entertain them until about five in the afternoon when our transport would come to take them back. We knew all these good people and I personally had enjoyed their hospitality often. Some worked in our local charitable institutions and some had officers and airmen billeted in their homes. They all agreed when Acton telephoned, so the plan went ahead.

By 5.30 on Sunday evening ten of the twelve US officers had arrived back at the Officers' Mess, but the two who had been invited to spend the day with Mrs M. did not arrive until 6.30. They were 'Stinko' and full of praise and affection for their hostess who had been so kind and generous to them.

This seemed to me a bit odd, because the Mrs M. I knew, and I had been to her house several times, would offer a small glass of sherry before lunch and maybe a glass of white wine with lunch. Nothing more. I made some enquiries and discovered that my adjutant had taken the name, address and telephone number of Mrs M. from the directory and had contacted the wrong one. One who was related by marriage but not exactly an inside member of the family. She was Austrian by birth and always kept a bottle at hand.

The time came when we decided to give a party for our local friends and to enjoy and repay hospitality. We had a splendid venue in Ashwick Hall which had been requisitioned as an annexe to the Officers' Mess. The problem was that the right Mrs M. who was well known to us, might take offence if she were not invited and had not been chosen to entertain two American officers, whereas a little known distant relative had. On the other hand the wrong Mrs M. had played her part magnificently and said *au revoir* to her guests, full of *bonhomie* and good spirits. The adjutant, Squadron Leader Acton, who had made the mistake was told that both the Mrs Ms would be invited and it would be his duty to keep them apart; they must not meet. He succeeded.

Queen Mary lived in Badminton House during the war as the Royal guest of the Duke and Duchess of Beaufort. Now and again she drove into Bath for shopping and relaxation, and on the way, along the A46 she passed an RAF guard-room with a notice 'Royal Air Force Station Charmy Down'. It was at the foot of a narrow lane leading uphill. She may or may not have known that it led to a very fine airfield with two long ashphalt runways. It was one of several hilltop airfields which remained operational while others lower down were fog bound. It was one of the four satellites of Colerne. She decided to visit Charmy Down so her equerry got busy.

He invited me to Badminton to arrange detail for the visit.

We agreed on a suitable date and time. We knew that Her Majesty should not be encouraged to climb into an aeroplane, especially a Hurricane, as she had done that before and it interfered with the schedule. I was at pains to explain that Charmy Down was a wartime satellite. There would be no Guard of Honour. The Camp Commandant, Squadron Leader John Mead would be present during the domestic part of the visit, and the senior WAAF officers would invite H.M. to tea with the WAAFs.

All went well. We flew a Mosquito in from Colerne, seven miles away. We rigged up a step-ladder and platform from which she could look into the twin cockpit of our most advanced night fighter.

She arrived with her son, HRH Prince George, Duke of Kent, who wore RAF uniform. I had met him before at Headquarters No. 11 Group Uxbridge, where he had access to the facilities in my office.

We stopped at one of the dispersal huts where aircrew on readiness lived and slept in their flying clothes. She drew attention to the little coal burning stoves which were provided for these huts. She tapped one with her famous umbrella and said, "These things were used in the Crimean war; you should have central heating here." In the car I was invited to sit between our two royal guests and as it was a cold day a warm rug was drawn over our knees. I was all nice and cosy as we drove round the perimeter of Charmy Down looking in here and there to inspect, to meet and to greet.

A few weeks after the royal visit to Charmy Down I received a signed photograph of Queen Mary addressed to me personally. I was in no doubt that it was intended for the whole station — but which one? Colerne, the parent station or Charmy Down the satellite? I decided on Colerne because I knew it would be exhibited there permanently. I had it framed and it was hung in the foyer at the entrance to the Officers' Mess. I am sure that it is still there. Some time later when I had returned to Bentley Priory I received a polite but accusative letter from the equerry at Badminton to say that I should not have kept the portrait for my own glorification (not his words). I wrote back a simple explanation and all was well. I think what happened was that somebody at Charmy Down at the time was so impressed by the friendly visit by H.M. to such humble surroundings that he or she wrote to Badminton and asked for a signed portrait. It was most probably sent, but Charmy Down today is farming land with a few derelict wooden buildings around.

CHAPTER XI

1944 and All That

Early in 1943 I was posted to Bentley Priory and I did not know why. I had been at Colerne for less than a year and it was unusual for the Commanding Officer of a large station to be replaced. I imagined it was to do with the detailed planning of the invasion, but that subject was not yet discussed in responsible conversation and I had not heard of 'Overlord' nor 'Bigot' until I had been back at HQ Fighter Command for several weeks.

Although most of the heads of departments were known to me changes were taking place and it was common knowledge that Sir Trafford Leigh Mallory would become Commander-in-Chief of Allied Air Forces Europe. In the meantime the war went on and Ops 3 played its part. That part was less important now, and the Head of the Department was downgraded to Group Captain. Since I was already his deputy, Air Commodore Embry put me in charge. Later he became Sir Basil and was decorated several times for bravery so it had been and was a pleasure to be on his staff. My last appointment in the RAF was at Fontainbleau in France where he was C.-in-C. Allied Air Forces, Central Europe in 1954.

Let us now return to our domestic scene at Stanmore, where I was joined by Jane, Bruce and also Anne. I rented a small furnished semi-detached house near Stanmore tube station, a ten minute walk from Bentley Priory. On February 25th 1943 our first daughter was born in the local maternity hospital and her name is Frances.

We had, in Ops 3, a very competent and amiable officer who came from one of the three London Auxiliary Squadrons based at Hendon. He was on the wrong side of the age scale which decided whether your services would benefit the nation better by being in the air or in an office. Also he was a founder member of Ops 3. His name was Squadron Leader Ralf Hiscox, known to everyone as 'Hicco'. He was a member of the Planning Committee for Overlord, attended all the meetings and kept me informed. I was consulted once or twice on matters relating to Air Defence, but spent more time dealing with the mundane matters of the day. After the war 'Hicco' was elected Chairman of the Council of Lloyds of London.

While Sir Sholto was still C.-in-C. there was the burning issue of the future of 'Turbine Lights'. These were Havoc (American DB7) aeroplanes which had been converted over here, by GEC, to carry in the nose and in place of the gun turret, a searchlight. This great light was powered by batteries stacked in the bomb bay. They were not the standard lead-acid batteries which were used in motor cars then as now, but nickle iron ones (knife batteries) which were heavier but could be charged quickly. Technically it was a masterpiece but it was a monstrous white elephant inflicted on Fighter Command from above.

Whenever a new concept. a new aircraft or new armament, was proposed for Fighter Command, it was customary for it to be evaluated by the FIU at Ford and attention to be paid to the report. A Havoc Turbinelite was sent there early enough to make the evaluation, which was not very favourable; there were three main conclusions, the first being that the performance of the Havoc was not adequate, its top speed being some 30 m.p.h. below that of a Beaufighter.

The second conclusion was that dependence on a second aircraft to provide the armament may be acceptable for a demonstration but not for a wartime situation. And last there was a recommendation that a Mosquito Turbinelite, with its own armament, be made available for an FIU evaluation of the whole concept of a searchlight in the sky. Meanwhile one DB7 each week was being converted at Burton Wood into a Havoc Turbinelite.

A base was established at Heston, near London Airport of today, with the full use of the airfield, a large hangar and other buildings. Ten Turbinelite units with their accompanying Hurricanes were deployed on night fighter airfields throughout the UK. The Hurricanes were there to shoot the bandit down once it had been illuminated by the Havoc.

The imbecility of this philosophy can be exposed if you try to kill a fly in a dark room with the help of a torch and a chum with a fly swat.

Several departments of the Air Ministry had been inspired to a high pitch of enthusiasm for the Turbinelite, undoubtedly by the Leigh Light which was being used with such success by Coastal Command against U-boats in the Bay of Biscay. Why not introduce and cultivate the same techniques to our night fighters? The aim and object were the same, to seek, to identify and to destroy the enemy.

On the surface a submarine could cruise at perhaps sixteen knots. It could dive also, but that was not a high speed manoeuvre. It operated therefore, in the horizontal plane only at 16 knots. A bomber of the German Luftwaffe could fly at 200 miles per hour and operate in both the horizontal and vertical planes. Why should these two prime targets for the RAF bear any comparison? They would both take evasive action, when threatened, but only according to their own fashion. Some sympathy and understanding must also be accorded to the pilots of the Hurricanes who were expected to fly in formation, in darkness, with their parent Havoc, through cloud and rain; often reaching the limits of their endurance, be it fuel, oxygen or just mental fatigue.

The climax came when the Air Ministry informed the C.-in-C. that plans were being discussed for equipping all night fighter squadrons with Mosquitoes, carrying searchlights, and if structurally possible to have their own armament. The C.-in-C. was asked to submit his opinion on the introduction of these aircraft into existing squadrons.

There had been a Turbinelite unit at Predannock when I was there and also one at Charmy Down when I was the Commanding Officer at Colerne, the parent station. Inevitably I knew the opinions of the pilots who flew these Havocs and Hurricanes and they were not at all favourable. I spoke to SASO who agreed that any one spokesman for or against the future of these units would be very vulnerable. He would, therefore, suggest to the C.-in-C. that all officers commanding Turbinelite units, should attend a meeting at Bentley Priory to give the users a chance to express their opinions.

Sir Sholto was an exceptionally intelligent man and very fair and experienced. The Unit Commanders assembled in my office and I made it clear to them that they should have no inhibitions about stating their views. We went from there to SASO's office and so to the C.-in-C.'s Conference Room. There SASO suggested to Sir Sholto that before we discuss the main item on the agenda and since, for lack of bandits, we had no evidence of the success or otherwise of Turbinelites, each one of the unit commanders should be invited to express his opinion.

There were none in favour although one or two thought that more trials and experience would be welcome. At the other extreme there were one or two who declared that if they were in radar contact with a genuine bandit, they would not put the light on at all but try to direct their limpet Hurricane into a position for visual contact and attack in the dark. They all wanted to fly Mosquitoes but preferred them without a searchlight.

A few weeks later the Turbinelite units were disbanded and all work, both experimental and constructional was cancelled.

There were two or three other unique projects which came under the wing of Ops 3 but only one of importance, namely the three 'Intruder' Squadrons. Their task was to cross into enemy territory to bomb airfields and attack German night fighters based there, while Bomber Command aircraft were on their way to or returning from their targets.

There was in Ops 3 a small office where Wing Commander Philip Lawton received information necessary from Bomber Command such as the target, the timing, and the route (or routes) of our bombers. He also received from our own Intelligence Section the airfields which were likely to be active and the enemy night fighter units based there.

Having collected and collated the information necessary for our intruders for that night he would issue, direct to the squadrons, the airfields to be covered and the time to be there.

The trouble with the intruders was how to assess their success. In the early days they had found enemy airfields lit up and aircraft in circuit taking off and landing, with navigation lights on. They claimed many successes and since there was no way of confirming or disputing these claims, the individuals were given the benefit of the doubt. Now in early 1944, the German night fighters did not show their navigation lights at all and the airfield lighting was strictly controlled. We had learned nevertheless some sobering and frightening lessons from the Germans because once or twice they sent a handful of JU 88s to mingle with our bombers, five hundred or a thousand of them, coming home to roost in East Anglia. Maybe our bomber aircrews decided that the risk of collision was greater than the risk of meeting a pike in a pond of goldfish. Most of them left their lights on and so did the airfields. Several of our bombers were shot down on each occasion but care was taken to ensure that no publicity was given to this lest the enemy be encouraged to increase its intruder missions.

Our intruders would have enjoyed far greater success if they had been equipped with our more advanced AI (Air Interceptor Radar). However, Bomber Command had requested and Fighter Command had agreed that none of our aircraft so equipped, would fly over enemy occupied territory, lest they should provide a weapon to be used against our bombers in the future.

Sir Trafford L. M. became Commander-in-Chief of Allied Air Forces Europe as well as C.-in-C. Fighter Command. With the tremendous influx of United States Army Air Force (USAAF) units, equipment, and high ranking officers he could decentralize his Fighter Command responsibilities to his SASO, now Air Vice-Marshal Geoffrey Ambler, and concentrate on the well-being and success of our joint Allied Air Forces.

L.M. had picked his own staff and the PA (Personal Assistant) was none other than James Leathart, my faithful friend in No. 54 Squadron, who had a problem and wanted to tell me about it. It arose when US Commanding General of the Ninth Fighter Force came to pay his respects. He had observed that his Commander-in-Chief had, for his personal use, a single engined aeroplane with only three seats. He, for his personal use, had a twin-engined Cessna built to carry six passengers. It was his wish that his C.-in-C. should have a Cessna delivered to Northolt. It would be a VIP one.

L.M. liked comfort but not ostentation or luxury and was very modest in his personal requirements. He consulted James Leathart, and explained that he would accept the Cessna, mainly because it was a matter of 'Hands Across the Sea'. He then told James to get rid of his Proctor (the RAF version of a Percival Gull) as he did not intend to build up a flight of aeroplanes for his own use. So the Proctor was returned to the Fighter Command communications squadron at Northolt for general use. No problem.

Several weeks later the US Commanding General of the Ninth Bomber Force came to pay his respects. He had noticed that his Commander-in-Chief had, for his personal use, a twin-engined Cessna which could carry six passengers. He himself had for his personal use a C47 (Dakota) fitted out to VIP standards and it was only right that his C.-in-C. should have the same. It carried 22 passengers.

Here again, for the sake of good relations, L.M. accepted and told James Leathart to return the Cessna to the USAAF with his thanks and appreciation. This he found impossible to do.

It was made clear to him by the staff of the Commanding General of the USAAF Ninth Fighter Force that the Cessna had become a war casualty and written off, as such, in Washington so it would be best for all concerned if its existence were forgotten. He went back to L.M. with this message but got a negative reply and therefore decided to make it his own personal aeroplane. He had JAL painted as registration numbers between RAF roundels and flew it wherever he went. He confided in me his anxiety whether he would be able to keep it or sell it after the war, or whether he should seek some charitable organization which would put it on an inventory. However, as we will hear later, it came to an honourable end on the 1st January, 1945.

Every now and again the C.-in-C. Bomber Command, Air Chief Marshal Sir Arthur Harris wrote a letter to L.M. complaining that Fighter Command was not doing enough to help his bombers with their offensive in Europe. In essence this was true because we had, in Fighter Command, a large number of aircrew and aircraft in squadrons not committed to any immediate or dangerous task, whereas Bomber Command suffered severe casualties every night of the week. What could we do to help, bearing in mind the restrictions and responsibilities which were imposed on our activities? The several suggestions made in these letters were, more often than not, impossible to fulfil taking account of the range, armament and equipment of our aircraft concerned, also the training of the aircrews.

L.M. was very occupied with his many duties and responsibilities leading to Operation Overlord so he passed the letters over to Geoffrey Ambler, his very competent SASO who, in turn, discussed them with me. Ambler telephoned Air Marshal (later Sir Robert) Saunby the deputy C.-in-C. Bomber Command, and arranged for me to visit High Wycombe where he and I could exchange our views and make suggestions and recommendations. This happened three times with no agenda, minutes nor anyone else present. In the course of these meetings we agreed on three very important matters for the present and for the future. The first was that there would be no attempt by Fighter Command to impose routing of outward or inward bound bombers, nor control of the use of navigation lights or airfield lighting, for the present. This might be reviewed if and when the risk from enemy intruders became greater than losses due to collision, faulty navigation or other emergencies.

The second agreement was the night fighter participation in the advanced training exercises in Bomber Command known as Bull's-Eye. There are two basic ways to penetrate a belt of concentrated night defence such as AA guns, searchlights, night fighters and the lot. One was known as the pheasant technique which the Nazi bombers had used when they attacked our cities here. They despatched each bomber at five minute intervals more or less, and each had the advantage of being able to take evasive action, and was not obliged to swim in the shoal. From the viewpoint of our defences, this technique meant tracking each bomber as an isolated target. If our organization, training, equipment, etc. were all perfect then we would expect one hundred per cent attrition rate against such raids; ten per cent would probably do.

The other basic way to penetrate a defensive belt is the partridge or mass raid technique. This is to pack together as many bombers as possible, accepting that some would inevitably perish and the rest get through to the target.

Of course these two descriptions are very over-simplified and there were many dissimilarities on both sides, but Bomber Command seemed to favour the partridge technique, and its crews were trained accordingly. Part of their training was participation in Bull's-Eye exercises.

These meant assembling as many training bombers (mostly Wellingtons) as possible and despatching them as a pack on a two or three point course over the lesser populated areas of Britain.

We agreed that our night fighters, under GCI control, would be fed into the pack to seek AI contact and follow these to visual ones, then the fighter would turn on his navigation lights and the bomber crew do the same. I believe that many of our night fighter and bomber crews benefited from Bull's-Eye exercises, although they were not a frequent event.

The other subject of our talks, indeed the primary reason for these meetings, was to explore what Fighter Command could do to help the bombers. We agreed that our task should be to take on the enemy defences over their own ground. To be successful this would mean co-ordinating our operations with those of Bomber Command. Our aircrews should be given the same briefing, the same criteria for weather restrictions, and the same authority for launching or cancelling each raid. It was also essential to co-ordinate the Radio Counter Measures (RCM) which had been developed separately by both Commands. It was agreed that at least five night fighter squadrons of Fighter Command should be selected and dedicated to night fighter support for the bombers. This meant that for operational purposes, they should be under the direct control of Bomber Command.

We were both thinking on the same lines but to get a clear picture of what we would recommend to our respective C.-in-C.s it was necessary to isolate any points of disagreement between us, if such points indeed existed. I had two to make, the first being the local reaction to the withdrawal of a night fighter squadron from the vicinity of a big city. Since our night fighter squadron had been based there no Nazi bombers had been seen nor heard, and the citizens feared that its removal would herald another blitz. A very parochial attitude but an understandable one, and one to be debated by and with the civic authorities.

The second was the removal of all restrictions on the use of advanced technology in our aircraft operating over the Continent. Bomber Command was already using, with success, very advanced radio and radar systems to pin-point targets and to enable the bombers to get to places five hundred miles away and attack them with precision. We in Fighter Command already had our GCIs and our squadrons were beginning to receive Mosquitoes equipped with AI Mark X. We concluded therefore that there should be no restrictions applied to the use of the most advanced radio and radar appliances which could be used to confuse or destroy the enemy defences.

A few weeks after this exploratory talk with Sir Robert, and while I was still in office at Bentley Priory, I was visited by Air Commodore Addison, who I had not met before but was aware of the predominant part he had taken in 'bending the beam'. He told me that a new formation was in the process of being established in Bomber Command to be known as No. 100 Group. Its purpose would be to help protect our bombers and it would have priority in the choice of ground and air equipment and personnel applicable to this purpose. He was to be the Air Officer Commanding (AOC) and would like my advice on the selection of his SASO. I had no hesitation in recommending Rory Chisholm who was then the CO of the FIU at Ford. His knowledge, experience and personality would be of very great value to the new 100 Group.

I was posted to 2nd Tactical Air Force (TAF) to be SASO to the AOC No. 85 Group and was obliged to concentrate my attention on the forthcoming invasion. I did not lose interest in No. 100 Group but it was no longer on my mailing list. It was not until the war was over that I learned how outstanding its success had been. In due course it became known that seven enemy night fighters had been destroyed for every one Mosquito of 100 Group lost, and this over hostile territory, sometimes 500 miles from home.

CHAPTER XII

The Invasion

It was inevitable that the basic plan for Overlord would be released soon, on a 'Need to know' basis, to those individuals who were to take part in the invasion and the follow up thereafter. I was therefore notified officially that I was to be SASO to the AOC No. 85 Group, and I was briefed on the structure of the RAF contribution to the invasion forces. I learned that No. 85 was one of the four groups which made up the Second Tactical Air Force under Air Marshal Sir Arthur Coningham; (to be known as 2nd TAF). Nos. 83 Group and 84 Group were to provide air cover and support to corresponding Army formations and No. 2 Group to engage in tactical bombing.

No. 85 Group was given no glamour role in which to shine. It was to be responsible for the administration of everything and everybody not immediately under fire nor likely to be. This included units such as base hospitals, transit camps, embarkation units, bomb depots, maintenance units and workshops, church units, rest centres and a multitude of others. It was to be responsible also for base defence, and this is where I come in. In Spain, in the Battle of Britain, in No. 11 Group and in No. 10 Group I had always been in places which had been under attack, but were no longer, and I fired my guns in anger only once. In retrospect I like to think that my appointment as SASO to the base defence commander must have ensured that our bases would not be attacked while I was there. With the exception of the incident on New Year's Day 1945 this was true, but I mention it in all humility.

In theory we had three Mosquito night fighter squadrons on our inventory, of which only one was based in France. We had also a priority claim on six day fighter squadrons, to be negotiated through HQ 2nd TAF. What we did have in practice were three GCI Units with a full array of communications and all very mobile. There was also a commitment to the American Forces to retain one squadron of night fighters including a GCI based in the US zone of the invasion area. The USAF, at that time, had no night fighters in operational use.

The AOA (Air Officer Administrator) was David Lane who was

given the acting rank of Air Commodore at the same time as myself. He was one of those outstanding entries to Cranwell from the Apprentice School at Halton; we had been Flight Cadets together in the same squadron. In HQ No. 85 Group he would find plenty to do in the administration of what was probably numerically the largest Group the RAF had ever known. He coped with this monumental task extremely well.

By mid May the headquarters staff of No. 85 Group were encamped in tents on the sports grounds of the RAF Depot (Uxbridge). It was there that the staff were ready to meet, greet and strive to be of service to the AOC once we knew who he was to be. We were aware that the senior officer first listed was critically ill and a replacement would have to be vetted, injected, briefed and selected, before being named and finally appointed.

It was with greatest pleasure and delight to me when it became known that Air Vice-Marshal Steele (later Sir Charles) had been chosen. He was once SASO in No. 9 Group and then AOC No. 10 Group, and while I was in charge of Ops 3 at Bentley Priory we met quite often.

One of the classic principles of war is to operate from a secure base but on June 6th 1944 the aim was to secure a base from which to operate and into which our men, armaments and supplies could come ashore and expand from there. We in No. 85 Group accepted the fact that an enemy air attack on our bases would be made under cover of darkness, because the extent of the air superiority we could exercise by day, both the United States Air Force (USAF) and the Royal Air Force was overwhelming.

The men and supplies required for the initial landings on D-Day were brought ashore by landing craft immediately on to the beaches and by floating quays provided within the sheltered confines of the Mulberry harbours. There was a limit to the capacity of these facilities, and indeed the invasion forces were dependent on them for several months to come.

No. 85 Group had few priorities but two GCI Units were phased in during the first ten days (say D + 4 and D + 8). One of these was established a few miles from the beaches in the direction of Caen and would give cover to the sea approaches from the north-east and the land approaches from the south. This was a unit especially designed for mobility. It was phased in on D-Day to its selected site, and was in operation on the first night. It was commanded by James Leathart and had a minimum number of personnel, which included an experienced GCI Controller and a liaison officer to co-operate with searchlights and AA guns. This unit was wearing RAF blue uniform and was easily mistaken for the enemy, so it became a matter of urgency that all RAF personnel were issued with khaki battledress.

The first objective of the invading armies, once the beaches had been secured, was to capture Cherbourg in order to have a deep water port with the quays and cranes needed to supply the Allied forces. It was the American Army which was to undertake this task supported by Allied air and sea power. Thus the site chosen for the second GCI was at the north-east corner of the Cotentin Peninsula and about twelve miles east of Cherbourg.

On June 21st, together with Brigadier Hughes who was in command of the anti-aircraft batteries, we flew from Heston to Airfield B6 in the invasion area. This was to be our future base, shared with two squadrons of fighter bombers of No. 84 Group. The runway was not yet ready and the surface was being prepared for the laying of PSP (Pierced Steel Planking) but landing the Auster was no problem. We were met by James Leathart, now Group Captain Ops at Headquarters 85 Group and spending a few days in Normandy to help our two GCI Units to settle in. He was also keeping an eye on the site allocated to No. 85 Group Headquarters when it arrived.

He told me that the second GCI Unit and crew had arrived and was waiting to be deployed and get into business. This was the one which had been committed to the American Sector and was to occupy an area of marshland and a large house near by which had been used by the Germans; there was a massive aerial on the marshland which had been destroyed by fighter bombers of the RAF. James told me that the US Commanding General, General Shram, had agreed with the CO of the GCI Unit, namely Wing Commander Bill Moseby, that an attempt should be made on June 24th to drive the four or five vans, all prime movers, to their allotted site on the north-east point of the Cotentin Peninsula. James and I decided we would like to go too and a Jeep was put at our disposal. We assumed that Bill Moseby had the US permits and intelligence reports, so on that day we joined the others. It was said that the road up the east coast of the peninsula was clear but we must go through Carentan as the direct route was flooded. The distance to drive to the site would be about 40 miles, not far provided all went well.

In Carentan everything seemed normal, considering it had been in the battle zone a few days before. The streets were full and the shops were open. Ten miles further on we went through a village where we were welcomed with flowers and bottles of wine. We were getting a bit anxious, because we had not been stopped at any road checks and there was no traffic whatsoever on the road. Another ten miles and we came to another village where all the windows were shut and boarded up and not a soul to be seen. I took a mental note of our armoury and could account for four Webley 0.38 revolvers, two in each Jeep, these being the mandatory equipment of officers in wartime. There may have been some rifles with the NCOs and airmen in the GCI vans following us but I do not think so. We were in fact defenceless.

Nevertheless we reached the large house (or chateau) without incident and found that it had been vacated by the Germans only a short time before. Electrical equipment of all shapes and sizes, documents and debris of every kind littered the place. We were aware that there may be booby traps but none were found.

We moved on to the marshland where the GCI was to be situated and left the vehicles and personnel there. James and I turned round and headed for home, but we decided to go into Barfleur, which was near by to get something to eat. We entered Barfleur in the early afternoon and found all the windows shuttered and nobody in the street. Obviously the usual precautions had been taken so we drove to what appeared to be the biggest hotel, although it was only a village pub, and knocked on the door. It was opened and we explained that we were RAF officers and we would like some bacon and eggs. The proprietor was nervous and excited and said, *"Oui, oui, monsieur, oui, monsieur — attendez, attendez,"* so we sat down to wait. We thought we were waiting for bacon and eggs, but in fact the proprietor had contacted the Mayor of the town and several other dignitaries so instead of bacon and eggs we found a mass of people waiting to see us outside the hotel and the Mayor and his council came inside and greeted us. They brought in two prisoners, who turned out to be Italians, and wanted us to take them away to a POW camp. We managed to persuade the Mayor that they had to stay where they were until the Americans came to take them away. We never found out whether Barfleur had been visited by American units or if it had been bypassed without the inhabitants being aware of the progress the Americans had made towards Cherbourg. What we did hear later was that our GCI Unit, on the marshland, was shelled next morning and had to be moved back quickly to the chateau. It is therefore apparent that we were fairly near the battle zone and had we continued any further would have run into enemy patrols, and not only enemy ones, but American patrols too, and would have found it very difficult to justify our presence in the battle zone. They would probably assess us as doubtful intruders. That all happened on 24th June. Cherbourg was occupied by the Americans and surrendered by the German Forces there on 26th June 1944. On the way back the windows were still shuttered and the shops and streets still empty. Although we had achieved what we set out to do, the expedition was foolhardy to the extreme and we were lucky to survive. Intruders we were, indeed.

Next day I was back in my tent at Uxbridge and was able to visit my wife and two children at Whitchurch.

By mid-July the staff of HQ 85 Group had moved from Uxbridge to the site where our tents had been erected in an apple orchard near to the B6 airfield. There was a cider press there with a family occupying it and a large house which was empty and badly in need of repair. Like so many of the country houses in Normandy, it was probably built in the eighteenth century. The drains were virtually non-existent and the two WCs had to be boarded up before we could go into the chateau at all. However, we did manage to use some of the rooms as offices and this gave us more space in the tented area near by.

We had two vehicles intended as mobile offices, and these could accommodate two of us, one on each side of the van. One of these vans was used by the AOC as his sleeping quarters and a private office. James Leathart and I shared the other van. Tents were used for all other purposes and the Officers and Airmen's Messes were surprisingly comfortable.

We were there during the period of intense fighting round Caen, about 15 miles away. Although we took no part in it, the congestion on the roads and the movement of men, supplies and munitions was very substantial. There was bitter fighting also in the American zone further west. These battles in the American and British sectors led to the breakthrough at St Loe and the tightening of the Falaise gap, culminating in the march on Paris. The Allied armies entered that city on 25th August 1944.

On that day, Bill Moseby, who was commanding the GCI in the American sector, telephoned me and proposed that he should take his GCI to Paris in order to give some protection in case there was a vengeance raid by the Luftwaffe on that city. He was full of enthusiasm, but had to get the consent of our AOC. I saw the AOC and he agreed with me that it would be a good idea, although not essential to the war effort, so I gave Bill Moseby the AOC's permission to go ahead. We both felt there was no point in trying to dampen Bill's keenness and it might be a useful contribution by 85 Group to the defences of the American sector, which now included Paris. Of course, everyone about us was infected by euphoria, which spread like a disease throughout the land.

Early next morning, an American aircraft landed at B6 and an irate General Shram stepped out. I was there to greet him — all smiles — but he wanted to see the AOC. On the short walk across from the airfield to the AOC's caravan office, he told me the gist of his complaint. It was that no one had consulted him, and the GCI was in the American zone for the protection of the American forces in the event of a night attack. Day attacks were extremely unlikely and they had their own defence equipment for them. Both the AOC and I had thought, but failed to check, that Bill Moseby had contacted General Shram before asking permission from us to move the GCI to Paris. We should have checked first, so we were entirely in the wrong, and General Shram was completely justified in his complaint. He spent half an hour or so in the AOC's caravan, and I hope they agreed on their differences, if differences there were.

The Germans were now in full retreat, and they left behind, particularly in the Falaise gap, all their heavy armament. They had lost thousands of men, killed, wounded and captured, and there seemed little possibility of further resistance. They had been badly mauled and were demoralized and disorganized and people were justified in thinking that this was the end of the war. So it would have been if the gap at Falaise had been closed. They retreated through France and Belgium and sought sanctuary in Germany and in Holland where, given time, they could re-form, re-equip and again resist the Allied pressure which was being exerted on them. The Allies had their difficulties too, and the principal one was logistics because men, munitions, supplies, petrol all had to come overland from the beaches in Normandy. Although Cherbourg had been in Allied possession for two months or more, it was still not open to ocean going ships. The sabotage there and the demolition of essential dock equipment, particularly cranes, also the mines in the harbour entrances, had all contributed to a very slow reconstruction, which ships would need before they could bring essential supplies in through Cherbourg harbour. Also in Allied hands but not operative, were the ports of Le Havre, Calais, Ostend and Antwerp.

Antwerp was the most important of these. Although it had been captured intact and was operational as a harbour, ships going there had to steam seventy miles between the port and the sea. The river Scheldt for most of its course, was dominated by German fortifications on the island of Walcheren, constructed as part of the sea wall against invasion, and very formidable. The island is on reclaimed land, one of the polders below sea level, so depends for its crops and its very existence on the dykes which hold the sea back from the pasture land on the island. Bomber Command undertook to destroy these dykes and let the water in to isolate the fortifications, I say isolate because the fortifications were built largely on sand-dunes, which were not below sea level. Bomber Command achieved this objective, and the whole island was flooded except for the fortifications along the coast and these put up a formidable resistance. The job of clearing them fell to the Canadians and they were successful but suffered severe casualties. The first convoy of Allied ships arrived in Antwerp harbour on 28th November. Soon after the fighting was over and the Germans had left Walcheren, mostly as POWs, the Chief Signals Officer of 85 Group, Group Captain Colin Stewart, suggested that I should accompany him to visit a small unit he had established on the north-west coast of that island. I agreed, and we transferred from our staff car somewhere *en route*, into an amphibian DUKW. We found the way by following the signposts which stuck out of the water two or three feet above the road. Our desination was a small hut on sand-dunes on the north coast of the island, which had not been flooded. From this hut there was a distant view of the west coast of Holland, and in particular that area from which the V2 rockets were being launched towards London. Day and night watch was kept with binoculars, and when the flame of a rocket motor was spotted, the transmitter was activated. This was a lightweight unit powered by a small petrol engine such as one sees on lawnmowers which transmitted a bleep on a beam to the UK, where it was relayed direct to the air raid warning centre at Bentley Priory. A V2 rocket took four minutes to reach London and therefore the good citizens had four minutes to find shelter. Perhaps not long enough, but what more could be done?

It did not take long for us to settle down in Ghent. We had excellent accommodation and an airfield, housing and overwhelming hospitality. It was, in fact, difficult to keep up with the number of invitations we got from our Belgian friends to meals, dances and parties, and there comes a time when you say "enough is enough" trying at the same time not to offend our hosts by refusing invitations.

Several disarmament units had been established under the administration of 85 Group. Their purpose was to render useless any armament the Germans had left behind. This was necessary in case the tide should turn against the Allies and the Germans reoccupy Belgium and Holland. These consisted of some ten to fifteen Belgians under the control of an NCO of the RAF and were engaged in destroying not only complete aircraft and other main items, but also back-up stores which could be of use to the Germans if they returned to this territory.

One day I was visiting one of these units which was operating in a large storehouse full of spare parts for the Luftwaffe. Items of all kinds were unpacked and hammered to pieces and thrown into a central dump and later would be buried. There were electric motors, altimeters, instruments of all kinds and raw materials such as dural panelling and rods and pipes, all being broken up and discarded. It seemed such a waste but it was necessary, not only to ensure that these items could be of no further service to the Luftwaffe, but to prevent them being sold after the war to undesirable clients. We had plenty of the same sort for our aircraft and other weapons and we could do without competition from German stores.

I was getting a bit bored with very little to do and my 'garage rat' instinct began to stir within me. Surely I would be able to use some of this equipment to make something practical? Several projects crossed my mind, but I decided to examine in greater detail whether I could make an electric motor car for my son Bruce. I listed the items which would be needed, and went back to the disarmament unit where I had seen similar items coming under the hammer. Nearly everything I would require was there, all brand new — batteries, electric motors, dural panels, girders — in short there was no major item of equipment that was not available in quantity. Next, I got the assistance of the senior engineering officer of 85 Group, and he gave me the use of a mobile workshop. This was a large vehicle which contained a lathe, drills and tools of all kinds, which would be required for my amateur engineering. I got the approval of the AOC to undertake this project and to park the mobile workshop at the back of our office building. He agreed that I might use an annexe to my office as an assembly room where I could fit the pieces and put the whole project together and it was not long before I started work.

One morning, in December 1944, while I was visiting our GCI Station at Eindhoven by car, I received a personal message from Air Vice-Marshal Teddy Hudleston, who was then AOC 84 Group, inviting me to lunch with him at his HQ at Tilberg, which was on my way back to Ghent.

I arrived there in good time and was delighted to meet my friend and contemporary from Cranwell days. After lunch he asked me to visit him in his office as he would like to discuss a matter in private. He gave me the sad news that my elder brother Alec (Fatty) had been killed in a flying accident at Biggin Hill.

Alec was a pilot for Imperial Airways when the war began, based at Nairobi, Kenya. He had served five years in the RAF on a short service commission and was called up and posted to Egypt. He then went on to India to become CO and founder member of No. 194 Transport Squadron, which became famous for its Flying Elephant symbol, and the squadron was known as 'The Friendly Firm'. It was the leading air supply squadron for General Wingate's Chindits and other units of the 14th Army fighting in Burma. He was awarded the DFC and the American DFC also. In 1944 he was posted to the UK and admitted to Uxbridge Hospital to be treated for malaria, which had been a chronic complaint for him. I visited him in the hospital, which was very close to our encampment, prior to the invasion, on the playing-fields of the RAF depot. On his recovery, he was posted as Chief Instructor to the Leicester East OTU of 46 Group, Transport Command.

In December, he flew to Biggin Hill on a personal visit which was to have lasted an hour. He had a navigator with him. When they taxied out to take off he did not notice that the elevator control lock was still in position. Despite this he became airborne normally and made a partial circuit of the airfield and approached to land on the runway, but the aircraft was in a nose-down attitude, and because of the elevator being locked, he was unable to correct this and bring the tail down. On landing, therefore, the Dakota pitched forward and the propeller of the port engine hit the runway, broke off and passed through the pilot's seat on the left hand side killing Alec, leaving the navigator unhurt. There have been quite a number of similar accidents in Dakota squadrons.

Teddy Hudleston very kindly loaned me an Anson and a pilot to take me to Biggin Hill and promised to send another Anson to collect me, at my request. My mother, who had lived alone in London throughout the war, was at the funeral at Biggin Hill. She was in great distress having lost two sons during the war. I returned to London with her and next day flew straight to Ghent in an Anson.

With regard to our working day, David Lane had the bulk of the work to do. Reconstructing our HQ with a different motive in mind — to create a more permanent organization and to cope with the many administrative necessities that occur. Units had to be formed, or brought from UK to cater for every branch of human life. My responsibility was base defence and particularly night defence, but since we were not being attacked either by day or night, except for the one incident on January 1st, there was little I could do in that direction, but we had other opportunities. Bomber Command now had No. 100 Group at its disposal, without any restrictions on the use of skills and equipment, its purpose being to minimize the number of casualties suffered by our strategic bombers. They were using the latest AI Mark X Mosquito aeroplanes and many gadgets designed by the boffins. We, for our part, moved our GCI to situations more appropriate to the task of 100 Group. It must be remembered that most of the aircrews and controllers came from Fighter Command and liaison was 100%. The GCI which had originally been allocated to the American Zone was returned to UK and our third GCI was shipped in and set up near Eindhoven in Holland. The original GCI which moved into Normandy went first to Amiens and operated from there for a time but was then set up at Louvain in Belgium. Both Eindhoven and Louvain were close to the front line and between them they could see most of the activity going on in Western Germany. They could vector the night fighter Mosquitoes of 100 Group to attack the German night fighters almost from the moment of take off. Take off signalled the approach of Bomber Command heavy bombers so the night fighters the Germans sent up were tracked right from take off until they mingled with the Lancasters and Halifaxes of Bomber Command. The control of 100 Group night fighters was exercised by liaison officers with us at Ghent and also with the two GCIs.

New Year's day, 1st January 1945, was in Ghent just like a Christmas card of a bright crisp and exhilarating winter day. I was walking with the AOC from our house to the office block when we were surprised and perplexed to hear the rat-tat-tat of machine-guns and then see some ten to twenty fighter aircraft, with swastikas, diving on our airfield near by. We hurried to the office block and up to the top floor where there was a good view of the airfield, which was completely undefended, no RAF Regiment, no heavy AA and no light AA.

The two squadrons of Spitfires based on Ghent airfield were under the control of No. 84 Group. These had left to take part in operations elsewhere and two of their Spitfires remained on the ground, probably being serviced. Also on the ground were an Anson, an Auster and the Cessna, with registration markings J.A.L. By the time we reached the top floor of the Headquarters building all five were ablaze. The FW 190s left as quickly as they arrived taking a reasonably direct route for home and suffering no losses so far. However, they had not reckoned with the AA belt which had been installed to protect Antwerp and Brussels from low flying aircraft and VI doodle-bugs. They did not know that the guns had been turned around to await their return, and were loaded with proximity fused shells. These shells had been in use in England, pointing out to sea, along the coast of Kent, to combat the VI doodle-bugs. They were very successful but their deployment inland was forbidden in the UK by the knowledge that if they did not explode in the proximity of an airborne target they would do so in the proximity of some highly populated piece of land in Kent.

The raid by the Luftwaffe on Ghent airfield was only one of very many similar raids made on the same day at the same time, on the Allied airfields in Belgium and Holland. They lost many aircraft in the air and we lost some on the ground, but ours were mostly small ones used for communications. All were replaced within two days, except one, the Cessna J.A.L.

It is, I believe generally accepted now that this supreme effort by the Luftwaffe was intended to establish air superiority, maybe only temporary, while the German offensive in the Ardennes was in progress.

I was feeling very contented and assured of my future in the RAF. I had become an Air Commodore at the age of 36 and had served on the staff of several senior officers who could shape my destiny. Then a terrible tragedy occurred which was to influence my whole future.

One evening towards the end of March, 1945, when we were having dinner in the AOC's house, the telephone rang and I was being called from Bentley Priory, Fighter Command. The caller was 'Hicco' who was in Ops 3 with me in Fighter Command and he had some urgent and unpleasant news for me. My wife Jane, whom he knew, had telephoned and asked him to convey a message to me. He told me that my son Bruce, aged 4½ years had been operated on for peritonitis and was in a critical condition in a nursing home in Reading. I asked 'Hicco' to let my wife know that I would be on my way home that night. I remembered there was a Mosquito on our airfield at Ghent and it was at our disposal. I knew the pilot well and he agreed to fly me to Hampstead Norris which was the nearest airfield to Whitchurch/Pangbourne. The AOC gave me his full approval to fly there and be away for several days. We were airborne within the hour and arrived at Hampstead Norris in good time.

There the Station Commander very kindly provided transport for me to go the ten miles or so to Whitchurch.

Amidst fear and general depression, Jane told me that Bruce had complained of a tummy-ache and this had become severe enough for her to call in the local GP. Jane suggested that it might be appendicitis, but he rather scoffed at this and put it down to 'green apples'. Next day Bruce's condition was so bad that the GP arranged for an ambulance to take him to a nursing home in Reading. The operation, they said, was successful, and there was an improvement in Bruce's condition during the next two or three days, but then he went into a coma and died on 18th April 1945. After the funeral, I returned to Ghent and started to work again on the electric motor car. There was less enthusiasm now but it seemed to me that it might give pleasure to my daughter Frances when she was a bit older. The main object was to keep my interest going and to prevent me becoming too morbid.

The AOC (Charles Steele), had been unwell on and off for some time. His trouble was a duodenal ulcer and he was posted back to the UK to undergo treatment. His successor was Air Vice-Marshal Dermot Boyle, who later became Sir Dermot and Chief of Air Staff at the Air Ministry. He was and is a unique personality with great charm and ability, he was very popular during the short while he was our boss at Ghent. I was still in Ghent when the Germans were driven out of Holland, leaving the population on the brink of starvation. We in 85 Group played our part with the distribution of immediate relief and making provision for long term supplies to be available to the population. It was in the coastal sites north of The Hague that V2 sites were located and although the weapons needed no launching pad they did have to be supplied with liquid oxygen and very pure alcohol, and it was the latter which aroused our interest.

It was there in vast quantities ready to be consumed or destroyed and somebody had knowledge of a distiller in Hamburg who claimed that given pure alcohol he could blend it into any liqueur or equally spiritual drink and it would be medically safe.

The Army claimed that the V2 was a piece of artillery and therefore they were entitled to the alcohol. We argued that it was a rocket or flying machine and therefore the alcohol was claimed by our disarmament organization. We won the argument because we had the tankers and these would be cleaned out and used for conveying the alcohol. The Army had no such vehicles.

The war ended on the 8th May 1945 and the way was clear to take our tankers to Hamburg and to arrange with the distiller to turn this alcohol into gin and bottle it. This was done and in due course it was bottled and labelled 'Bad Eilsen Gin' but it became better known as V2 gin! It was retailed in Officers' Messes, Sergeants' Messes, and wherever there was a bar which served drinks, the retail price being two shillings a bottle. Of course, a number of us would take a bottle or two home when we went to the UK, for there were no Customs then, and we didn't sell it but we gave a party for our friends who had been 'gin-deficient' for a very long time. The bars, etc., which retailed this gin made enormous profits to be ploughed back into the Mess accounts, and enabled us to buy more expensive drinks, such as whisky, comparatively cheaply.

In late June, I took a fortnight's leave and met Jane and Frances at Rhosneigr in Anglesey. It was a seaside village highly recommended to me by James Leathart, and it had a night fighter airfield at Valley, immediately adjacent to where we had booked rooms in the local hotel.

CHAPTER XIII

Peru Revisited

While I was on leave, I discussed with Jane the pros and cons which would be facing us in the near future. To reach higher rank, i.e. Air Marshal and above, it was essential to be nominated to and selected for a six months course at the Imperial Defence College (IDC). There I would meet and compete with officers I had known well for many years, some of whom I liked or disliked, some who liked or disliked me. To go to the IDC and not be promoted to higher rank would be a great disappointment.

The alternative to pinning my hopes on going to the IDC was to plan to spend a few years in a land of plenty, which had not suffered the ravages of war, and where sunshine and friendship would encourage us to settle down, increase our family and have a happy home life. My erstwhile friend, Freddie West, was now incumbent of the DDAFL post at the Air Ministry, so I went up to London to see him and to find out whether he had any vacancies in the Air Attaché world, preferably in South or Latin America, where my Spanish would be useful. He told me there were two coming up shortly, one, Air Attaché to Buenos Aires, Argentina, and the other in Lima, Peru. If I were to be posted to the one in Argentina, I would keep my acting rank of Air Commodore. But a complication was that both my wife and I were born in the Argentine, and according to their law, those born there were Argentine citizens. They were expected to travel on an Argentine passport, to do military service, unless exempt, which I was. All my Argentine papers were in order, but so were my British ones and no such complications would arise, if I were to be posted to Lima, Peru. I would not be without friends and contacts in Lima, as I had been an instructor at their cadet college and was an accepted member of the British community there too.

I told Freddie West that I could foresee difficulties and suggested that the Foreign Office should be consulted before the selection was made. Freddie agreed and we left it at that, so B.A. or Lima would be our future desination. As it turned out, I was posted to Lima, the Air

Attaché selected for B.A. was born in the Argentine too, but he did not tell anybody.

Back in Ghent everything was topsy-turvy. Plans which had been drafted to ensure a smooth and successful transition from a wartime to a peacetime condition, were being applied to both the military forces and the civilian population.

2nd TAF had been disbanded and the central point of control was BAFO (British Air Force Occupation). The HQ was at Bad Eilsen where there was plenty of accommodation and an airfield. The C.-in-C. appointed was Sir Sholto Douglas and his SASO Air Vice-Marshal Charles Steele. I was to be the deputy SASO and was given an office in the same block. WAAFs were posted in to do secretarial and other jobs which they did in UK. Plans had been made for married quarters so that officers and airman could have their families there and live together in reasonable comfort. In short, the whole of the occupied area was being converted from a military one to a civilian one. The same transformation was being applied to the German areas in order to get people back to normal working conditions and to reconstruct their country with the aid of the Marshall Plan. I had spent a few weeks in Ghent waiting for my posting to come through, closing up my office and dealing with the correspondence of the day, but I had not forgotten my little 'pup'.

I worked on it and reached the stage where it could be driven, but no bodywork had been done. Panel beating or 'tin-bashing' as it is known in the RAF, is a highly skilled trade and I was not going to attempt to learn it, I therefore got the 'pup' ready for transportation to Bad Eilsen. It was unfortunate that I could not get anyone small enough to drive it to see whether the engine and other components were working properly. It was too small to be driven by a grown-up person, so I made arrangements for it to be sent to Bad Eilsen as soon as I was ready to accept it there and I would then decide how and when it could be fitted with a body.

In Bad Eilsen I was a member of the Senior Mess and President of the Mess Committee. I took advantage of this because I wanted to work on my 'pup' and there was only one garage for the Mess. As it was not in use and not really needed, because all the cars there were housed and serviced in big transport units and three which were chauffeur driven were kept elsewhere. So it was that I was able to use the garage for working on the 'pup' and to keep it there. I made enquiries about the possibility of having the bodywork done by professionals and discovered there was a small workshop, or factory, in Dortmund which specialized in 'tin-bashing' and made the cowlings and gun turrets and other similar things for the Dornier aircraft of the Luftwaffe. I went to see them and found a lot of Germans hanging around with nothing to do; they were only too pleased to take on this job and worked enthusiastically on it. A fortnight later I was able to go to Dortmund again and found a magnificent job had been made of it. Obviously I could not pay them in cash as we were not allowed to use the German currency and all our transactions were in paper notes called BAFs, but they were very pleased when I handed out several tins of cigarettes. Back in Bad Eilsen I was able to exhibit the 'pup' to my friends and colleagues, who had taken an interest in my engineering. One day the C.-in-C. came to look at it, and no doubt was pleased to see that a member of his staff was usefully occupied during his spare time.

About this time, the C.-in-C. sent for me to speak to me alone in his office. He told me that he would nominate me for selection to the IDC and suggested that I should go there to fulfil my career in the RAF. I was most surprised and honoured that he should consider me to be such a worthy member of his staff. After all, Sir Sholto was perhaps the most experienced, respected and enlightened of the top echelon of the RAF, and any nominee of his would automatically be selected. I expressed my gratitude to him and asked if I may give an answer after discussing it with my wife Jane, and also with my immediate superior, the SASO.

Jane, I knew, was enthusiastic about going to Lima to start a new life there. If I were to go to the IDC based in London, I would have to find accommodation, adapt myself to service life once again and I knew my limitations. I had no real ambition for higher rank and so, after a reasonable time, I explained all this to the C.-in-C., who saw my point of view. I had been a member of his staff on two occasions and he respected my opinion.

Before I left Bad Eilsen, I made arrangements with the officer in charge of transport for the 'pup' to be sent to the UK and then on to Liverpool to be loaded in the SS *Santander* outward bound. It seemed that the Customs were most suspicious when the crate was unloaded in the UK. They suspected that it contained an 'object of loot', when coming into the UK, and a secret weapon when going out! The crate was opened on both occasions, so it was just as well that the declaration of the contents were verified.

Jane and I enjoyed the voyage, although it was not all plain sailing. There was a hurricane in mid-Atlantic, and the ship had to go south by the Azores to avoid it. We had engaged a nanny for the journey and to help during our appointment in Lima. She was confined to her berth, being seasick, all the way from Liverpool to Havana — 11 days. The *Santander* was on her maiden voyage, she was basically a cargo ship, but carried twelve passengers. Accommodation was very comfortable, but she was not a luxury ship and loaded and unloaded at various ports in the Caribbean and the Pacific. I have always been fascinated by the sights and sounds one enjoys on deck going through the various stages of the Panama Canal. The voyage took about three weeks in all and we were met in Callao by Group Captain Harger, whom I was replacing. He assured me there would be no problems with the Customs and that I would enjoy diplomatic status. He had chosen a house for us, subject to our requirements, but meanwhile we were to stay at the Country Club. The house and the Country Club are very close to each other, in the best residential disrict of San Isidro. I was grateful to Geoffrey Harger for arranging our accommodation.

My first responsibility was to meet those people I had to work with, both in the Embassy and outside. The house he had recommended was just what we wanted, it was a small, modern house in the garden district of San Isidro, with four bedrooms and three reception rooms. There was a servant's bedroom and about a quarter of an acre of garden with an automatic watering system. It was rented furnished, the furniture being of good quality, and we made it comfortable and it suited us. The Country Club, close by, was a meeting place for friends and was a convenient place to stay for three weeks until we got our belongings sorted out and moved into our house, which remained our home until we left three and a half years later.

It was now time to take stock of the matters on which I would be expected to report both to the Ambassador (Mr Roberts, later Sir Walter) and the Air Ministry, and bring myself up to date with the latest situation in Peru.

On 7th December 1941 Japan decimated the US Pacific Fleet lying in Pearl Harbor. For a time there was little naval protection of the west coast of America, North or South, and it was feared that the Japanese would land and establish a base, and where better than Peru? With its predictable climate, several excellent harbours, and above all, abundant oil supplies with a refinery on the coast, the base could be used to attack the Panama Canal and, who knows, creep up into Mexico and California. Peru had become a country of strategic importance to the defence of the Western world and USAF was quick to act.

Airfields were built with proper runways, USAF squadrons were based there, instructors were sent to train the CAP, and selected officers of CAP were sent to the United States for advanced training. Existing units of the CAP were equipped with modern aircraft required for defence.

I had now returned to Peru in late 1946 as Air Attaché to the British Ambassador in Lima. I was accredited also to HM Ambassador in La Paz, Bolivia. I was provided with a motor car and an aeroplane, neither of which was new. The car went under the name of 'Cars Passenger Heavy'. It arrived camouflaged, had enormous desert type tyres and gun racks. I did have it painted black and fitted with CD plates, but all the same, it looked a trifle ludicrous when lined up with the large shining American limousines belonging to other members of the Diplomatic Corps. There was some compensation in that it was an extremely reliable Humber, and once outside the city could compete with any other car on rough roads and shifting sands. I drove it once from Lima to La Paz, which took five days each way.

The aeroplane was an RAF Dominie (i.e. a DH Rapide). My predecessor had taken delivery of it and nearly lost his life crossing the Andes direct from Lima. Its fabric drooped down like an offertory bag, and it was fitted with a radio which no one could operate or undestand.

I did however, get it across to Eastern Peru by flying first up the coast to Chiclayo and then crossing the Andes at 15,000 feet only, but I admit that I was scared of flying it, except along the coast. Eventually the CAP came to my rescue and Dick Vigil, by then the CO of the workshops at Las Palmas, offered to refabric and refurbish my Dominie at a price which was agreed in London. It finished up by being the best Dominie in the whole wide world, but then I was told that it had been disestablished, so I must sell it. It went to a buyer in Chile.

It is difficult to define what an Air Attaché does to justify his appointment and the high standard of living that goes with it. There were, at that time, and perhaps still are, several explanations given by representatives of Ministries and Departments to justify the presence of an Air Attaché in any country. It is the Treasury in the end that has the last say, although Air Attachés are paid from RAF funds. To give some examples of the reasons for an Air Attaché to be appointed to any one country, I suggest the following:

(1) To enhance the glamour of the retinue of HM Ambassador on social and ceremonial occasions, by the presence of his Air Attaché in full dress uniform with gold braid, epaulettes, medals and decorations, renowned for his good looks and social graces! He must

be prepared to offer and receive abundant hospitality even from comparative strangers, to an extent beyond the normal call of duty. An attractive and intelligent wife is also an asset. These attributes apply almost exclusively to the prestige capitals, such as Washington and Paris.

(2) To report to the Ambassador and the appropriate branch of the Air Ministry on all matters connected with aviation in his appointed country, both military and civil, which may be of interest and may need action.

(3) To assist and support the agents and visiting representatives of the British Aircraft industry in the many ramifications of that industry.

(4) There were, and probably still are, several countries which are friendly and dependent on the UK and where RAF missions or individuals are employed as advisers. In such countries the Air Attaché becomes an avuncular liaison officer between the mission and the Government of the country concerned.

In Lima I found the most important matter with which I had to spend a lot of my office time concerned civil aviation. Firstly, and where I could give some immediate help, was the advent of BSAA (British South American Airways). Of course I knew that BSAA intended to implement a route down the west coast of South America, calling at the capitals of several republics, such as Bogota, Lima and Santiago. There were many potential passengers who wanted to fly to Europe, and had pounds sterling or other European currencies, but no US dollars. All existing air fares across the Atlantic had until then to be paid in US dollars and BSAA would obviously benefit by accepting payment in European currencies. Although a temporary agreement had been arranged with BSAA for them to use Lima airport (Limatambo) yet no preparations had been made for handling passengers or for the use of the ground facilities, so it came as a great surprise to us in the Embassy in Lima when we learned that the west coast route would start operations and the first aircraft would be arriving in two weeks' time. There was no BSAA representative in Lima at the time and no office and of course everyone was knocking at my door. However a few days later a gentleman came to see me and told me that he had been appointed BSAA Manager in Peru and asked for my help, which I was only too ready to give. There was a lot to be done to provide the ground and air organization to serve scheduled flights, especially long distance ones. With the approval of the First Secretary I arranged to have an Embassy office on a temporary basis for BSAA and all correspondence and telephone calls must be addressed to that office.

A problem which caused a certain amount of acrimony, was the supply and installation of the equipment and communications for flying control and navigation. All existing radio and communications were owned and manned by Pan American Grace Airways (Panagra) which was the prime user of these facilities, and other civil aircraft visiting Lima were obliged to pay Panagra for the use of their flying control network. That seemed to be reasonable and BSAA should have accepted it but they wanted the Peruvian Civil Aviation Authorities to provide ground services which were appropriate to the equipment carried in their aircraft. It was not long before the problem was solved, because the International Civil Organization Authorities decreed that standard procedures and equipment must be provided for use by aircraft of all nations flying on international scheduled routes. The first Lancastrian arrived on time and I was there to meet it. Both the passengers and crew were very tired for it had been a long flight, but I felt that they were not properly equipped. The aeroplane had left UK in the middle of the winter there in Britain. It arrived in Lima in the middle of the tropical summer and the passengers looked none too happy. Whether any arrangements had been made for them to change into tropical clothing and to keep their overcoats stored somewhere *en route* I don't know.

A few weeks later, an advertisement appeared in the Peruvian *Times*, inserted by BSAA Headquarters in London. This paper was the English speaking newspaper of those days. The advertisement was headed 'Fly British, Fly Safe'. On the same page in the same issue of the newspaper there was a report on the accident rate of all international airlines operating in South America. BSAA had by far the worst record. I think that the headquarters of BSAA in London thought that I was ganging up against them but in fact I was trying to help them. My reports went to the Air Ministry and the Foreign Office and I expect extracts from them were sent on to BSAA. I got plenty of co-operation in Lima itself, but I was not popular at their headquarters in London.

Later in the year two delegates were sent out by the Civil Aviation Authority to discuss a request by a newly formed airline company which was negotiating for an air route from Peru through to New York or Washington and on to Canada, with a possible extension across the Atlantic. This company which was called Peruvian International Airways (PIA for short) was financed in the United States and was seeking approval from the UK authorities for two stopping places in the West Indies with full rights to pick up passengers and to land them at one or other of the Caribbean Islands which were under the Colonial Office in London. This was in accordance with the terms of the temporary bilateral agreement which had already been signed by the Peruvian Authorities and UK. The First Secretary of our Embassy in Lima was nominated to be a member of our delegation and so was I, so there were four of us present at all the meetings. The Peruvians nominated their Foreign Minister, General Revaredo, who was their Foreign Minister and a Senior Member of the CAP. He spoke excellent English and knew a great deal about civil aviation and all the ramifications thereof. Also nominated was Colonel Villegas who was the Solicitor for the Foreign Office. At our first meeting all went smoothly and it seemed there would be no problems. The Peruvians agreed to BSAA being nominated as the British Airline going through Lima. The Peruvians nominated two islands in the West Indies, say Jamaica and Trinidad, and it seemed that there would be no difficulty, but of course our delegation had to get the approval of the Civil Aviation Department in London. When we got back to our offices a signal was drafted to London recommending that the two islands nominated should be part of the agreement. It was several days before we got a reply and this reply was not at all satisfactory. The two islands nominated were not approved and the reason given was that they did not constitute a reasonably direct route between Lima and the destination of Washington or New York. This seemed nonsense but the Peruvians agreed to nominate two other islands. Again these were not approved for the same reason and we concluded that the authorities in London did not wish the new company PIA to operate this route at all, and after some informal conversations with our friends in the United States Embassy in Lima we deduced that the reason was quite simple to understand if explained simply and clearly. It was that there existed between the US and Canada on the one hand and the West Indies on the other, a very lucrative tourist trade and the islands of the West Indies were served by airlines both US and British. To allow Peruvian International Airways to run a service picking up and landing passengers *en route* would be detrimental to the existing enterprises. Moreover, to permit Peruvian International Airlines to do so, similar applications would no doubt be made from the other countries in South America who had routes to the United States and Canada.

Negotiations had been delayed quite a long time by this lack of understanding with London. However, when explained to the Peruvian delegates they accepted this explanation and did not try to retaliate against BSAA. The agreement was then signed and ratified in London.

A few weeks after arriving in Lima I decided that the time had come to give the 'pup' an outing. It was still in the crate which had remained unopened in the garage since we arrived.

Just around the corner from us was the home of Phillip Barker-Benfield, the Public Relations Officer at the Embassy and his family included Simoncito (little Simon) a proper little extrovert who feard nobody nor anything be it animal, vegetable or mechanical. I let it be known that the 'pup' was about to be unpacked so he came along with half a dozen other spectators. It did not take long to open the crate and Simoncito was in the driving seat in no time pressing every button and tugging or pushing at every lever. He was demanding to go. Since the batteries had been sent away for charging I could not oblige but it took a lot of persuading and some bullying to get him to go home. When he did go he gave furtive glances over his shoulder to make sure that nobody else had usurped his entitlement to be the test pilot. A few days later the two batteries were installed and Simoncito was behind the steering wheel, again raring to go. The road in front of our house was a cul-de-sac with very little traffic all moving very slowly.

Nevertheless the 'pup' got off to a fine start. Phillip and I had to run to keep up with it as the car swerved from one side of the road to the other. Obviously Simoncito was giving the steering mechanism a good test. Then it stopped as suddenly as it started and I knew at once that the trip switch which I had fitted in preference to a fuse had cut out the electric motor. I switched it on and we tried again several times but every time it cut out after about 20 seconds, so I decided to postpone the test and put my toy away in the garage while I thought over its future. Simoncito was furious and reckoned he had been cheated.

With regard to mechanical remedy this gave me no cause for worry because the problem could be solved easily by fitting a trip switch with a higher capacity or by altering the gear ratio. There was, however, a much more serious anxiety to consider.

When I first decided to embark on the conception of a toy motor car for a five-year-old powered by electric batteries, I had in mind that I would be based in the UK where I could find a disused airfield with runways and hard standings, or perhaps parade grounds or private drives where I could let a child practise the circuit and bumps without any anxiety. But here in Lima there were none of these facilities available and also there was no workshop at my disposal. In brief, it was too much to expect a child of five to know the highway code and rules of the road, and there was no environment in which he could exercise his skill as a test driver to the full.

A few blocks away from our home there lived an Italian engineer who I had known in 1935 when he was in Peru at the service of the Caproni company to supervise the assembly and delivery of the aircraft which that company had sold to the CAP. He had stayed on in Lima thus avoiding the war and had established a very lucrative business building fishing boats in Callao, where he had been financed by a wealthy Peruvian, Señor Ferreyos. The engineer, whose name was Sacerdote, enquired whether I would like to sell my 'pup' as he wished to give it to Señor Ferreyos as a present for his grandson, aged five, who would be able to practise his driving on the roads and paths in the park garden of his grandfather's estate.

It seemed to me to be wise to accept this offer although it was only for a few pounds. My Italian friend assured me that he would take care to make it safe and sound mechanically, and after some show of affection I said goodbye to a small bundle of metal which had kept me interested and active for many months.

I never heard or saw anything of my 'pup' again. Simoncito kept walking up and down the road to make sure that no one else had taken his job from him.

There are many places of interest in Peru that should be visited but the roads, especially in the mountains, are rough and narrow and very often non-existent to those places one would like to see. Moreover, they could be very dangerous especially in the mountains. I will record two narrow escapes which have haunted me ever since. The first was on a return journey across the mountains behind Lima. I had been to San Ramon which is a small airfield on the eastern foothills of the Andes. It is at about 4,000 feet and where the jungle gives way to woods and green patches. To get there by road one has to drive up the valley behind Lima and reach the plateau at about 15,000 feet. Actually the rail and the road from Lima cross at 16,000 feet. Having crossed the plateau one arrives at a small town called Tarma. It is here that the downward journey begins and the road is so narrow in places that there are 'up' days and 'down' days but no question of being able to overtake. For much of the way the road is confined to a track cut into the precipice which extends some 1,000 feet above and an equal sort of distance below, and there is little opportunity to look up or down. I was on the return journey from San

Ramon to Tarma where I was to spend the night, and with me was a personal friend Charles Huntley Robinson. We were on an 'up' day and we followed a lorry heavily laden with oranges. When we came to one of the turning points the lorry driver turned in and waved us past, which was a very kind gesture particularly at that point and unusual with the lorry drivers in that part of the world. We continued on the road which was cut out of the precipice and was only wide enough to accommodate one vehicle. Suddenly there was a patter of small stones hitting the roof of the car and it gave us great cause for alarm. There was nothing to do but drive ahead as quickly as possible to see if we could get into a safer area, it was the only alternative. The precipice on which we were hanging turned to the left and we went across there as quickly as we could and the track turned round to the right and we reached a point where we could see where we had already been, and an amazing sight met our eyes. It was a landslide of gigantic proportions with rocks the size of houses coming down the precipice, some bouncing on the road. We decided that we were in an unsafe area and drove away still on the side of the precipice, as fast as we could. When we reached Tarma we informed the police so that they could warn other drivers and close the road. They must have succeeded in doing this because no vehicle was caught in this landslide. I was particularly concerned about the lorry driver, but it seems that he was the other side of the danger zone. The road was closed for six months but an engineer, who came to make plans for the reopening of the road in due course, was killed, I assume he fell over the precipice. Charles and I returned to Lima very much shaken by our experience.

The other occasion was on my return journey by car from La Paz to Guaqui which is on Lake Titicaca and it is the port where the rail from La Paz ends and all traffic is taken by steamer to Puno. This is the normal way of travelling but my car was not acceptable on the steamer and I wanted to explore the coast road. This road is not used a great deal and there is no traffic to speak of, an occasional clapped out old car or lorry every half-hour or so. It follows the shores of the lake round to the south-west side of it and is never very far from the main water. The total length of the lake is about 150 miles but the road keeps more or less alongside the lake. Every now and again one passes a small ford where water from a stream crosses the road which is always visible on the right side. I had been warned and heard tales of the dangers of these small streams because they are fed by the surrounding mountains which are very high, almost 20,000 feet and when there is a storm in the mountains the amount of water coming down becomes a torrent, when some 6 or 8 feet deep of rushing water would carry an ordinary vehicle away to its disappearance in the lake.

Having crossed one or two of these streams I arrived at one rather bigger than the others and I wondered whether I could negotiate it. It was no more than 40 feet and it did not look deep so I decided to have a go. I should add that I was on my own which is rather stupid in that part of the world but some arrangements I had made for a companion to come back with me had fallen through, so off I went into the stream in my faithful Humber thinking that if anything could get through that stream my Humber would be the first. I got to about half-way when the engine spluttered and stopped and it was very obvious that water had got into the exhaust pipe and there was not much I could do about it. I thought of how I could abandon the car, what I could do to raise help and every other thing one thinks of in desperation and fortunately I had an inspiration. I remembered how I had seen cars driving off their batteries in garages, so I tried this. I put the car into bottom gear and I pressed the self-starter and to my relief and amazement she went forward and we came out the other side. I spent half an hour or so drying the distributor, removed the plugs and let her dry out. It started up and apart from a few coughs and misfires got under way and I was really lucky to have survived. I don't know whether there was a torrent on that particular day or in that stream, but the threat was always there and as I say, I was very lucky to get away on my own.

In mid 1948 I was told that I was to return to the UK at the end of the year as I had been selected for appointment to the DDAFL post at the Air Ministry. My successor in Lima was to be Group Captain 'Finco' Finch who would arrive in time to take over from me. This gave me the opportunity to vacate my house and make preparations for my departure and also to introduce 'Finco' to the 'goodies and baddies' in Lima.

When I called on the Air Minister to bid him farewell, he told me that it was customary to decorate the Attachés of other countries accredited to Lima with the Air Force Cross, Second Class, at the end of their period of service. However he knew that the Foreign Office in London would not allow British Attachés to accept such decorations. I was aware of this, but reminded him that I had served as an instructor to the CAP (Peruvian Air Force) and it had been declared publicly that I was to be presented with the Peruvian Air Force Cross, but I had never received it. The Air Minister was surprised at this and undertook to investigate it, while I for my part would seek the authority of the Foreign Office in London to accept this decoration for my services with the CAP in 1935/6.

The outcome was that later on I was invited to the Peruvian Embassy in London to receive my Peruvian Air Force Cross, but First Class this time, from their Ambassador. There were several old friends there and a good time was had by all.

So it was that five of us returned home in considerable comfort in the flagship of the PSNC *Reina del Pacifico*. There were five because my second daughter, Jill, was born in Lima in March 1947 and my son, James, in September 1948.

CHAPTER XIV

Deputy Director Air Foreign Liaison (DDAFL)

I had never held office in DDAFL before, nor indeed in any other Department of the Air Ministry, however, it was well known to me because in all my special appointments overseas, it was DDAFL who selected me and I was briefed, administered, praised, rebuked by his department, and in return I sent my reports to him for distribution and action where necessary. So now I was to be DDAFL himself and responsible to the Assistant Chief of Air Staff (Intelligence).

I would have on my staff three Wing Commanders to concentrate on events happening in specific foreign countries on a global basis, and a number of Squadron Leaders and Flight Lieutenants who were specialists of one kind or another. There was also, the never-to-be-forgotten J. B. Hogan, the senior Civil Servant, who had been the backbone of the branch ever since anyone could remember. All officers, NCOs and airmen sent to foreign countries as Air Attachés, advisers or for other special duties, were dependent on J.B. for their indoctrination and subsequent welfare. J.B. would make appointments for them to meet leaders of the aircraft industry, to visit their factories and to call on appropriate departments of the Foreign Offices, there to meet selected executives and to learn what would be required of them.

J.B. was very proud of the young persons and personalities who had gone through his hands, and he kept one wall of his office decorated with their photographs. He never failed to remind them that the Air Ministry was not an RAF Command, and that the Secretary of State for Air was the Air Minister, and all RAF personnel serving there, were just his advisers. Few of us serving officers were aware of this and tended to think of the Chief of Air Staff as the 'boss man'. J.B. and DDAFL could and did work in close harmony so long as they respected each other. I intended to keep it that way. DDAFL enjoyed a special privilege. He was the only RAF officer serving at the Air Ministry, other than members of the Air Council, who was allocated a chauffeur-driven car for his own exclusive use. It seems that many years ago, a wise and sympathetic senior officer, or it may have been a Civil Servant, became aware of the considerable risks incurred by DDAFL and members of his staff from becoming victims of their own physical weaknesses through being required, by nature of their duties, to spend many evenings 'eating and drinking for Britain'. This they did to an extent beyond the normal call of duty.

In order to reduce this danger, he proposed to higher authority, that a chauffeur-driven car should be established in the department, and such was the logic of his reasoning that it was readily approved and DDAFL has had the use of a car ever since. I found that I was allowed to extend this privilege to members of my staff and to ACAS (I), but retained control myself. The car would meet me at Victoria Station at 9 a.m. every morning and take me to my office in Monk Street, Horseferry Road; not far, but I was now living in Cuckfield and the fast train from Haywards Heath carried many interesting and important people including Mr Harold Macmillan. I never knew him, but touched my cap to him like everyone else.

It took me some time to discover that now and again my chauffeur would go on the 'bash'. This was brought to my attention by one of my staff, and I had no alternative but to report him to the Civil Servant in charge of transport, and he was transferred. I was told, but whether it was true, that some Embassies had a private car park at the back, where the chauffeurs waited until they were called forward. One Embassy in question extended its hospitality to those men, serving them free drinks in liberal quantities while they waited.

My department was expected to arrange for the foreign Air Attachés in London to attend national events and ceremonies of importance, and to provide them with invitations and reservations. These events included the Royal Tournament at Earls Court, Trooping the Colour at Horseguards Parade, the Air Display at Farnborough and sporting events such as Wimbledon. So it was, that I was told about two weeks beforehand, that my department would be responsible for the reception and seating of members of the Diplomatic Corps at the presentation of the RAF Colours in Hyde Park, and that His Majesty King George VI would officiate on this occasion. A few days before the event, I learned that I would be in charge of the Royal Enclosure and would be assisted by a very glamorous WAAF officer and a highly decorated Wing Commander from Bomber Command. My assistants and I were on the site in the morning and it was raining steadily with a forecast of more to come. The Royal Enclosure was under cover except for a small dais which would be used for taking the salute. As forecast, the rain got heavier during the afternoon and we heard that His Majesty would be unable to conduct the ceremony. This was indeed the first public intimation that he was not well. The burden of presenting the Colour and taking the salute would fall on HRH Princess Elizabeth, our present Queen. One of my staff made a suggestion that we should send two officers in uniform to visit the big hotels in Park Lane, which were close to the scene of the afternoon's events, and that they should ask the Commissionaires, who conducted guests to and from their cars, if they could lend us some of their big umbrellas, of which they should have a plentiful supply. We had a very friendly response and they lent us all the umbrellas we needed. When the ceremony began, HRH Princess Elizabeth was expected to move to the small platform to take the salute, and this was not under cover. The Air Minister opened his umbrella and stood behind her to give her some protection, but he himself got a good soaking. One of the Royal party, Princess Marina, then Duchess of Kent, beckoned to me and asked whether the Air Minister would like to borrow her umbrella, but he declined. By the end of the ceremony, the weather had improved, and as the guests were leaving, a Squadron of Meteors flew over in formation.

The Air Display at Farnborough was always a trying event for DDAFL and his staff. The Society of British Aircraft Constructors (SBAC) sent invitations based on an official list which included VIPs from foreign countries, both military and civil, and representatives from their aircraft industries. Our Air Attachés contributed to these lists through DDAFL and were instructed to send to my office the names and addresses of those they thought should be invited. On receipt of these lists, DDAFL would contact SBAC, and request that the names submitted should be sent invitations direct to the persons concerned. SBAC would decide which of these persons should be invited to the President's tent for lunch. By collating these returns, a rough idea could be established of the numbers of people expected each day. We took comfort, however, in that the majority of the guests from overseas were invited by companies in this country who applied for tickets on their behalf. The first five days of the Air Show were reserved for official guests, the Services and all those taking part in the display and the general public were admitted for the final two days.

The difficulty we experienced in DDAFL was that several VIPs turned up with little or no notification and expected to have appointments arranged for them to meet senior officers, politicians and other people connected with aircraft business and have time set aside for this. I have in mind an incident in which I was involved in 1951. I had arranged with the Argentine Air Attaché in London for him to make a routine call on the Air Minister, Arthur Henderson, on a date convenient to them both. Two days before that date, the Chilean Air Attaché in London telephoned me to ask for an appointment for the Commander in Chief of the Chilean Air Force, who had just arrived in London to attend Farnborough, and would be here for three days only, to meet Lord Tedder, the Chief of Air Staff. After a lot of checking and rechecking, the Air Council Office offered me the same date and time as the reservation already made by the Argentine Attaché. After discussion, we decided between us that both interviews could take place at the same time as they would be in separate offices, and this was agreed and confirmed.

On the morning in question, both the Argentine Air Attaché and the Chilean Commander in Chief arrived punctually at the Air Ministry and Lord Tedder and Mr Henderson were at their desks to meet them. I decided to take the Argentine Air Attaché in to see Mr Henderson first, because I thought he would be able to speak English and secondly because the routine interview should not take long. Usually these routine interviews were a question of introductions and a five minute chat. However, on this occasion, the Argentine Air Attaché concerned could speak very little English and the Air Minister asked me to stay to interpret. When I eventually left his office, I was confronted by a very irate Chilean C.-in-C., who said he was not accustomed to being kept waiting and that he too was a very busy man. When we went in, I introduced Lord Tedder who apologized for keeping the C.-in-C. waiting, but said there was no need for me to be there as he also could speak Spanish. The meeting turned out to be a very friendly one.

There were two problems which I encountered during my time as DDAFL, which must have been known to my predecessors, but nothing appears to have been done to solve them, and so I decided to bring them to the attention of the authorities. These problems usually became exposed during the month or so of indoctrination which every candidate for an Air Attaché post underwent and more so perhaps when he was being interviewed by ACAS (1) and myself.

The first concerned the emoluments he would receive to enable him to maintain the high standard of living expected of every Air Attaché and his wife. No doubt he had heard of Air Attachés going into debt and in at least one case becoming bankrupt while still on duty overseas.

This was an easy one to answer, because a remedy had already been applied and I knew from personal experience. When I arrived in Lima in 1946 to take over my appointment there, my predecessor warned me that I could not possibly live or exist on the current pay and allowances, and he had managed to do so only because he was single and did not keep a home, but lived with friends as a paying guest. During the first year, I found out how right he was, but I was not unduly alarmed because I had managed to save up during the war. Moreover, I had a good reason for being optimistic. The turning point was, when a Treasury official arrived in Lima as part of a global assessment of payments to service Attachés overseas. In due course, when the review had been completed and the recommendations made, approved and implemented, I received over double that which I had been receiving before. Attachés would, in future, receive the same pay and allowances as corresponding ranks in the Diplomatic Service. If he could not live on this nor could the Ambassador. At the time when I was DDAFL the good news had not penetrated through the RAF and dismal tales still persisted. The remedy surely was to use some means to propagate this news.

The other inhibition which gave them cause to doubt was the knowledge that there were several ex-Air Attachés who had done two or more tours of duty as such, and when they returned to normal General Duties the AOCs and C.-in-C.s did not wish to employ them because they were out of touch with the current trends, both in administration and operations. My suggestion was that the officer in charge of postings in the Department of Personnel should not accept any officer who had done a tour of duty as an Air Attaché to do a second tour in the same rank, either acting or substantive, and should avoid also a second tour which ran concurrently, but in a higher rank. Pressure from the Foreign Office to override this rule should be resisted. To encourage candidates to seek some compensation for no longer being acceptable for second tours of duty, it was suggested that an ensignia or token of some kind should be worn or recorded against his name to indicate that the wearer had completed a successful tour of duty as an Air Attaché.

In the autumn of 1951 I was told that I was to be posted to RAF Kai-Tak, Hong Kong and would be CO of that Station. I looked upon this posting as very complimentary because Kai-Tak was such a busy station with the Korean war going on and activities all over the Far East. We chose to travel by sea and looked forward to the journey.

CHAPTER XV

Hong Kong and Kai-Tak

Early one morning in February 1952 I woke up lying on my bunk in the troop-ship *Dilwara*, three weeks out of Liverpool. I was travelling with my family and we were approaching Hong Kong. It was cold, but my cabin steward had brought some blankets for all our beds. The Officer in Command of Troops on board, who was host at our dinner table, had warned us of the sudden drop in temperature which would happen at this time of year when we were 100 miles from Hong Kong. Whereas in Singapore and other tropical areas of the Far East the temperature changed very little between seasons, in Hong Kong there is a cool and pleasant dry season and those expatriates who live in other countries of the Far East spend their holidays there when they get leave and if they can afford it.

I lay on my bunk thinking how little I knew about the evolutions and revolutions which were the current state of affairs in the Far East. I knew that North Korea had invaded South Korea and were having initial successes in their campaign, I knew also that Soviet Russia was supplying arms to North Vietnam to assist in a rebellion against French Colonial rule in Indo-China. I knew that the USA were sending forces to assist the French and also that the Communists were very active in Malaya but were contained by the British Forces there. These were but some of the many countries in the Far East which had been left without any administration whatsoever when the Japanese surrendered so suddenly in September 1945.

I was yet to learn that Mao Tse-tung had entered Peking and had declared himself the President of the Chinese Peoples Republic. Chiang Kai-shek had fled to Formosa, now known as Taiwan, and had taken the remnants of his supporters with him. He had declared himself President of the Chinese National Party.

The failure of the Nationalist Commanders to establish a firm line of defence south of the Yangtze or in the north-west caused the British, French and American Foreign Ministers to release individual but similar Press Statements on September 17th to the effect that their

Governments had found no Nationalist groups in China which were worthy of support. This declaration had a profound bearing on our future in Hong Kong.

In the first place the population of Hong Kong had more than doubled during the last two years. This enormous increase was the result of the remnants of Chiang Kai-shek's followers establishing themselves in Formosa but in order to get there they had to seek transportation from Hong Kong. It was therefore not a permanent increase but one that left its impact on the colony. In due course the Communist Army manned the check-point of entry and the boundaries, and forbade any Chinese without proper permits from entering Hong Kong from Communist China. This did reduce the inflow of refugees from Inner China, also it appeared that the Communist Republic did not intend to assault Hong Kong nor to change its structure to any great extent, but looked upon it as a gateway between Inner China and the rest of the world and encouraged large institutions to invest their money in Chinese enterprises.

One of the many problems which was facing Hong Kong and the rest of the Far East was the lack of sufficient transport. I refer in particular to the shipping problem. The changing situation throughout the area demanded a large quantity of shipping for the movement of supplies, munitions and above all, men. There were British Forces personnel in Malaya and India who had done four or five years' service instead of the normal two, because they had been unable to get a passage home. It was whispered that there were cases of mutiny but these had not been publicized. Hong Kong was a deep water harbour and one of few in the Far East. The only other one available in China was Shanghai, but even there it could not take the biggest ships which used to unload in Hong Kong and transfer their freight to smaller ships. For this purpose very large warehouses (godowns) were available. In the air too there was a big demand for transport aircraft and in 1951 Kai-Tak airport handled 5,200 aircraft movements and some 75,000 passengers. Today the figure is of course much bigger and the airport has been extended to cope with modern air traffic.

And so it was that at dusk that evening, we were steaming into Hong Kong harbour. We could see on our port bow the lights of Victoria, which is the town on the main Island, and on the starboard side we could see the town of Kowloon in the New Territories. I was watching the picturesque scenes in the harbour and the enormous amount of shipping and activity with small boats, but I heard in the distance, and then nearer, the sound of machine-guns and artillery and this persisted. No one seemed to be at all alarmed except myself.

We sailed into the godown area (that is the Chinese word for the quays and docks) where we tied up prior to disembarkation. I was pleased to be greeted by the AOC Air Commodore David Bonham Carter, whom I had met before but did not know well. I asked him why these machine-guns were firing in what was otherwise a peaceful surrounding. He was aware of my anxiety whether fighting was taking place and explained that it was the Chinese New Year and this was a normal custom. The machine-guns were fireworks and so were the bombs!

My family and I got VIP treatment going ashore through Customs to the AOC's car. He explained on the way to our accommodation that there was no CO's house in Hong Kong for the Station Commander and that he was obliged to offer me either a fairly large flat high up in a six storey building or two smaller flats on the same floor of a much smaller building; we decided on the latter. As a Station Commander I would normally have four or five servants, but servants were only allocated on the grade of accommodation and I had to make do with two. The servants are an important factor in Hong Kong because the HK Government wanted as many Chinese as possible to be employed to reduce the gross overcrowding in the colony due to refugees from the war in China. We had sufficient accommodation and servants to live a happy life but were unable to entertain. Next morning I was called on by Willie Devass, the Wing Commander in charge of administration at Kai-Tak. He had come to show me round the station and to give me a brief idea of things that needed my attention. He would explain the division between the Civil Aviation and the RAF stationed there. He would also point out all the different units and businesses which occupied the airfield. We drove on the road that ran alongside the perimeter of the airfield. The first thing I noticed was a battered old fence that anybody could get through, which formed the boundary of the airfield and on the other side of the fence, all the way along the length of the road were aircraft, large ones, in different states of repair and all looking rather scruffy; there were also many packing cases which were stored outside the hangars. There were three hangars also full of civil aircraft and spare parts. Willie explained to me that civil aircraft and spare parts belonged to the Chinese National Airline and that there were 26 aircraft all told, which had been serviceable when they were taken there two years ago. As they belonged to the China National

Aviation Corporation the Government of Chiang Kai-shek was anxious to get them moved to Formosa but there was a lot of controversy over this which I will explain later. We went first to the Officers' Mess where I was introduced to several officers who were off duty. It was an informal meeting. From there I went to Station Headquarters and saw the very comfortable office which was to be mine with a balcony overlooking the airfield. In spite of the geographical restrictions imposed on Hong Kong, flying had been taking place there since before the First World War. Before that they launched airships and balloons from the same site and flying boats and seaplanes operated from the waters of the harbour. Between wars the airfield was used by the Royal Navy to accommodate aircraft from the carriers based there. The geographical limitations which restricted the take off and landing at the airport were due to the surrounding hills which came right down to the perimeter of the airfield and rose to about 1,000 feet. Thus there was little or no room to manoeuvre when coming in to land and directly after take off. There were two runways when I was there, each being just under 5,000 feet long; too short for the large four-engined airliners which were then entering service. The runway which ran from the north-west to the south-east was used almost exclusively and in both directions, the south-east boundary of this runway extended into the water of the harbour and the approach that end was reasonable. Consequently it was used both for landing and taking off irrespective of the weather. This needed very skilful flying control.

One of these problems was that the hangars were in a direct line between flying control and the busy end of the main runway and the Controller was unable to see aircraft at the beginning of their take off or after landing. Another problem was the availability of alternative airfields for use in an emergency. The nearest one was Clark Field, the USAF airfield in the Philippines, this was 500 miles away. Most of the civil aircraft landing at Hong Kong came from either Singapore or Tokyo and both of these airfields were over 1,500 miles away. If therefore a diversion became necessary owing to the airfield at Kai-Tak being out of use, then the Controller must take action as soon as possible to divert all incoming aircraft to Clark Field.

The RAF presence at Kai-Tak was one squadron of twelve DH Hornets and a few miscellaneous aircraft such as one dual Mosquito, one dual Meteor, a Vampire, two high flying reconnaissance Spitfires, a Harvard and a target towing Beaufighter. There was also a detachment of Sunderland flying boats from Singapore and these came and went from time to time, but two were usually anchored in the harbour adjacent to the airfield. There was a satellite airfield, closer to the border, where a squadron of Vampires was based.

With regard to buildings, there were quite a number of new ones going up which was in keeping with the Hong Kong Government's policy to employ Chinese labour. The existing buildings which were brick built were the Station Headquarters, Workshops, Sick Quarters and the Officers' Mess. The buildings under construction, or approved for future construction were the Sergeants' Mess, Canteen and Airmen's Barrack Blocks. All these buildings were on the north side of the main runway and between runways there were the three hangars which I have already mentioned. These were intended as shelter in the event of typhoon and were there to protect all the RAF aircraft in the Colony. However, when the 26 aircraft of the National Aviation Company appeared on the scene, the Government insisted that as much protection should be given to them as possible and they had priority in the hangars. There were few aircraft in there, it was mostly taken up by packing cases full of spares. The plan was that if we were alerted to face a typhoon, we should take all our aircraft off and fly them to Clark Field or some other airfield which would not be subject to typhoon winds. Whether this could be done would depend on the amount of time which we would need to carry out such an operation.

The Hong Kong Government was particularly anxious to get rid of these aircraft which had become a 'hot potato'. The court case brought by the Communist Party claimed that these aircraft had belonged to the National Party Government which was no longer recognized by the United Kingdom as the *de facto* Government of China. Therefore the aircraft and accessories should be transferred to the lawful Government of China. The Communist Government of China won their court case and instructions were given to prepare to transfer the aircraft to some destination as yet unknown in inland China. However, the National Party, acting from Formosa, put in an appeal which was based on the fact that the Nationalist Government did not own the aircraft as the company was financed by private investment in the United States. The Nationalist Government won its case and one morning very soon afterwards I saw an aircraft carrier, albeit an old one, lying off Kai-Tak in the harbour and lighters going backwards and forwards taking on board the aircraft and equipment. The operation was done very quickly and if it were not for the extra space available on the airfield one would hardly have noticed the absence of these planes.

The AOC had his residence on the island facing south over Repulse Bay. It was a new house and a very attractive one, and the weather on that side was usually better than in Kowloon. The AOC's office was in the same block as the office of the Commander British Forces, General Sir Terrence Airey and the Naval Liaison Officer. The AOC was on his last appointment in the RAF and spent much of the time arranging for his future. Also, he was unwell for part of the time so I was acting AOC for many weeks, even months. It suited me because I got the run of the Marine section and could visit the Headquarters using the fast motor boats which were based there. The Headquarters had an Ops Room which was fed by two GCI Stations, one facing east and one facing west. Both these stations were on the mainland.

Some time before I arrived in Hong Kong there was an incident which involved the AOC and caused a certain amount of merriment. He was invited to a fancy dress party on the Kowloon side and this meant crossing by motor boat. He was dressed as a Chinese pirate and had arranged for his motor boat to pick him up at a small port on the island from where he could be taken across to Kowloon. The motor boat that was to pick him up was late and he paraded up and down the beach in his fancy dress clothes. Pirates still exist in that part of the world although they do not attack big ships any longer but they do have feuds and they are active against dhows and sampans. They are subject to arrest by police. Someone saw the AOC and believed him to be a pirate so the police were alerted. They came in force and insisted that the AOC was under arrest and would have to go to the police station with them in the Black Maria. He would be under guard. No amount of protesting on his part would make them change their minds, so in due course he was taken from the police cell to the Magistrate, who recognized him and the whole matter was forgotten.

There was in the space between the two runways a small engineering company named HAEC (which stands for Hong Kong Aircraft Engineering Company) financed and owned by Buttersfield & Swire and Jardine Matheson. Its clients were primarily small airlines which were based at Hong Kong or which had a major commitment there and required overhauls, maintenance and repairs to be done. This company earned an excellent reputation throughout the Far East for the quality of its work and for being punctual with its deliveries. The French, whilst they were in Vietnam, used it for the maintenance of their air force.

In chapter 4, I confessed that I had survived two 'prangs' during my 27 years service in the Royal Air Force. The first one was the event of 1932 when I was instructing at Digby and flew my Atlas into a tree, demonstrating to a pupil the art of low flying. The second prang was at Kai-Tak.

I did not do a great deal of flying while I was there, but just occasionally, say two or three times a month, I would go up in one or other of the aeroplanes of my choice. On this occasion, I was flying a dual Mosquito. I was quite experienced on Mosquitoes as they were the standard night fighter aircraft. In the dual Mosquito there are two levers that look exactly the same, and are just next to each other, say six inches apart. One raised and lowered the undercarriage, and the other controlled the radiator, which cooled the glycol used for engine temperature control. In the hot weather in Hong Kong, it is essential that the temperature control is operated immediately after landing, otherwise the glycol will boil and vapour will surround the aeroplane.

On this occasion I made an extremely good landing, I thought, and started to taxi, intending to lower the radiator, but I pressed the wrong lever and the undercarriage began to fold up under me. The plane sank slowly towards the tarmac and nothing could be done about it. My one thought was to get clear as quickly as possible, as there is always a fire risk with an engine still running. I had been given permission to land by flying control, and they were asking me on the RT whether I was clear of the runway, as there were other aircraft waiting to come in. The Controller could not see me because the hangars that I mentioned previously were in direct line of sight, and as I was disconnected I could not reply by RT. Wing Commander Hearle, the Senior Technical Officer at Kai-Tak, saw what happened, and with great presence of mind, commandeered a bulldozer, which was being used by a contractor near by and with it, scraped the Mosquito off the runway to a place where it would not be a hazard. The runway was clear again in less than fifteen minutes.

As for me, I adopted a penitent attitude as I walked slowly back to the flight office carrying my parachute, which seemed to weigh a ton, passing small groups of officers and airmen working on their aeroplanes on the tarmac. They exchanged furtive glances, but no one spoke a word until I was inside, where I was received with words of genuine sympathy and good wishes for the future. One bright young Pilot Officer exclaimed, "Well Sir, you observed the legend that every CO of RAF Kai-Tak has a prang during his tour of duty there." I was never able to check on it, but I did establish that one of my erstwhile predecessors flying a Vampire, landed on the short runway, overshot and finished up upside down in the drainage canal which carries the sewage of the town of Kowloon to the sea. He escaped unhurt, but has retained a faint aroma of roses ever since!

In addition to the civil aircraft which visited Hong Kong on scheduled flights, there were similar aircraft carrying service personnel to spend their leave in our Colony. One morning, I was watching a 4-engined DC4 approaching from the sea to land on the main runway. It came in very low, the starboard wheel hit the sea wall, whereupon the starboard undercarriage unit disintegrated and the fuselage scraped along the edge of the runway until it came to rest, fortunately, the right way up. It caught fire immediately. All this happened within 100 yards of my office and I ran downstairs towards the burning wreck. I was not the only one, plenty of people were around including the Station Warrant Officer (SWO). The door was opened from the inside and the passengers began to jump out one by one. There was no time to put down the steps, the SWO went to the door and helped the men as they jumped down from about six feet to be handed over to ambulance men who had just arrived on the scene. After twenty men had jumped, no more seemed to be forthcoming and the SWO climbed into the cabin to check whether there was anyone else inside. He was unable to get far because of the flames. His hands and face were slightly burned, but he was able to reach the ambulance and was taken to the sick quarters with the other passengers. Here it was found that all the passengers and crew had been accounted for, and apart from the SWO, there were no casualties. The American authorities sent transport for their personnel, who had been very lucky to have such a near escape. A few weeks later, I was pleased to receive notification that the SWO had been awarded an American decoration for bravery.

There were many VIPs who arrived in Hong Kong, some to do business but most of them in transit. We also had Royalty on two occasions, and naturally a Guard of Honour was required. At Kai-Tak we had a squadron of the RAF Regiment which was manned by airmen recruited in Malaya. They were very proficient at arms drill and it was standard practice to let them provide the Guard of Honour. However, I did have representations from our own airmen that they could provide the necessary skills and would like to have an opportunity to display them. Consequently I organized a special squad of selected airmen who would provide alternative guards as and when the occasion arose. They would be given time off from their normal duties to train for these events and I was very pleased with the result. I had always thought that airmen disliked drill and looked upon it as a form of punishment.

Although no active work had begun on the new runway, plans were being drafted and a committee had been appointed to approve these plans, and to supervise the work which would soon commence. The AOC was a member of this committee, but as he was so often away or not available, I had to attend the meetings several times. The Chairman was Sir Arthur Morse, the President of the Hong Kong and Shanghai Bank, an extremely able and powerful personality.

It had been agreed that the existing runways should be kept in service and the new runway on a new site running into the harbour. A channel was to be cut out of the rock which surrounded the present airfield and this would be lined up with the proposed runway running into the harbour to provide a length of approx. 10,000 feet. The ballast, which came out of this channel, would be used to build up the runway as it progressed into the deeper part of the harbour. There was not much for the RAF representative to do, although he was consulted on each occasion. Sir Arthur was particularly anxious that all radio and radar requirements should be provided and that we should anticipate new installations which would be required in the future. He made it quite clear that finance was no problem and we must make it one of the most modern airports in the world even if one of the most difficult to construct. Work was begun and the airport was opened on schedule. It is a most worthy tribute to the Colony.

I have already mentioned how delightful the dry season can be in Hong Kong, so it is only right that I should say something about the wet months, which are most unpleasant, and few visitors come except on duty. The temperature is not abnormally high, at about 90°F., but it is a damp heat which persists day and night with no respite except for the occasional tropical storm, which drenches the whole colony. It is the season when disease and depression are rife and little is achieved. We had to put the children to bed under mosquito nets with a fan directed on to their bare bodies in order to get them to sleep, but as this practice was discouraged by the medicos, we turned off the fan before we went to bed ourselves. In the early days of the Colony, casualties and the high death rate were such that few of the trading company executives completed their ten years' service out there. The chief culprit was typhoid fever, then known as enteric, closely followed by malaria. However, most of the well-known ailments, such as cholera, yellow fever, etc., were also present. Now, in our time, these diseases have been eliminated or controlled by drugs and inoculations.

Two remained which appear to be endemic to Hong Kong, namely 'sprue' and Hong Kong blisters. Sprue is a form of gastro-enteritis and Hong Kong blisters are small ones which contain pus. In both cases patients run a high temperature and seldom recover until the weather changes. Some improvement in casualty rates was noted when it was made obligatory for all airmen, working out of doors, to wear sandals, shorts and dark glasses — no headgear at all. All these ailments are greatly reduced, or eliminated altogether when buildings with offices and sleeping accommodation are fitted with air-conditioning units. We tried at Kai-Tak to get air-conditioning for the sick quarters, but because there were none readily available, and it all had to come from the US, it was not approved. Our small sick quarters had two wards with eight beds in each. During the hot weather the number of casualties grew considerably and the patients released became few and far between. At the peak of the period while I was there, the casualty rate was 18% of the total manpower.

When I took an aeroplane for flying practice, I usually went to our satellite airfield at Se Kong. This airfield had a single runway which was fairly narrow. The Vampire Squadron was based here and they had a happy little community, being the only unit on the station. They had a few administrative personnel, who did the domestic work, also the flying control personnel. I went there once or twice for guest nights, which I thoroughly enjoyed, but decided to stay the night rather than to risk the drive back.

In January 1953 I was promoted to the substantive rank of Air Commodore and informed that I had been appointed Assistant Chief of Staff (Intelligence) ACOS Int. to the Commander-in-Chief Allied Air Forces of Central Europe. It sounded rather important but I could not imagine what I would have to do in order to deserve such a splendid title. However, nobody seemed to be in a hurry to benefit from my services so I opted to go home by sea. I made reservations in the largest, fastest and most comfortable of the four troop-ships which plied the route to the Far East. I have forgotten her name, but she was built by Hitler as a 'Strength Through Joy' ship for the Hitler Youth Movement. She was due to sail from Hong Kong in two weeks' time, homeward bound.

However, a few days before we were due to embark, my elder daughter Frances was taken to hospital with amoebic dysentery and would be in quarantine for at least three weeks. I cancelled my reservations in the German ship and booked in the next troop-ship which was the SS *Andes*. She had been the flagship of the Royal Mail Steam Packet and was renowned for deck space and comfortable cabins.

By now the new AOC had arrived and taken over from Bonham Carter and my replacement had also arrived and taken over from me at Kai-Tak so there was nothing much to do except to be patient and wait, but we were still out of luck because before we were due to leave my wife was taken to hospital with measles and was too ill to travel.

We finally got away in the oldest, slowest and least comfortable of the troop-ships, she was called the *Empire Trooper* and during the next voyage she sank!

CHAPTER XVI

Allied Air Forces Central Europe — Fontainbleau

Nobody could justify the existence of AAFCE, and yet it had been a necessary organization at one time, when it was a repository where officers, mostly senior ones from five nations could be kept until their retirement, assuming that would take place before too long, or if awaiting promotion. The C.-in-C. was Air Chief Marshal Sir Basil Embry, who knew it was his last command before retiring, I also knew that it was mine, because I had declined nomination to the IDC. There were one or two RAF officers who were expected to reach higher rank but only one American in charge of a department, namely General Hale, who was ACAS (Ops.) The Deputy C.-in-C. was Air Vice-Marshal Pat Fraser.

No one knew for certain the true convictions of the C.-in-C., but outwardly he claimed that AAFCE was a fighting HQ, an integral part of NATO and he advocated it should play an active part in all operations and training exercises in the central area. In these declarations of intent he was supported by his Deputy.

The American members of the staff paid little attention to any plans and were convinced that the HQ was unnecessary and I think most RAF officers, other than those already mentioned agreed, as did the Canadians. The French, with few exceptions, were uncooperative and felt peeved that another HQ should be based in their country. The Belgians had a few representatives, mostly senior officers who were surplus to requirements in their own country. They seldom voiced opinions on operational matters.

I had on my staff a Group Captain RAF, a Colonel and a Major of the USAF, a Canadian Wing Commander, a Belgian Major and a USAF Captain.

In NATO all operational units answered to the Supreme Commander through their parent commands. In common with some of the other heads of departments, I tried to introduce special tasks which could be undertaken by my staff. For example, I put the USAF Captain on to targeting in our area. He became very enthusiastic about this, but all the data he needed on which to base his selection of targets, was already available at Supreme HQ and came from RAF or USAF sources.

The Group Captain RAF on my staff was a very discouraged officer because he had held recently the acting rank of Air Vice-Marshal and expected to go further in the RAF. At Fontainbleau he had been down-graded one rank and informed he would be retired at the end of his appointment there. He refused to do any work and spent most of his time out of the office. The American Colonel took much the same attitude, he thought all that went on in Fontainbleau was quite useless (maybe he was right!) and he had no intention of wasting his time — he put his feet up and read a book most of the day, taking no part in any of my plans. The other departments had the same story to tell. In brief, we were an HQ of considerable size, with no operational or administrative units under our control. As far as I could see, there were no plans for any specific role for AAFCE in the event of war. However, we did have a most comfortable environment in which to live and spend our time with our families. The offices were built to American design and very modern. The only complaint we had was that the very powerful heating was radiated through the floor, and rubber shoes of any kind were inclined to get hot and sweaty. The office blocks and canteens were on the outskirts of the Palace of Fontainbleau gardens while the married quarters, which were multi-storeyed flats, were on the other side of the town and very convenient for shops and schools.

Excellent sports facilities were available, and entertainments were laid on frequently in the evenings, bingo sessions being particularly popular.

I was allocated a large American car for my personal use, complete with chauffeur, Corporal Palmer, who was in civilian life a truck driver in Chicago. In the RAF, service cars were not available for private use, but it was noticeable that many of the other senior officers used their service cars for personal trips particularly to Paris, thirty miles away. Corporal Palmer was very upset that we could not go too!

I could have occupied one of the flats I have mentioned, but my predecessor had lived in a street, just near the Palace, named Dry Tree Road (rue de l'arbre sec). This was once the approach to the equivalent of Tyburn and the dry tree was the gallows at the end of the road. The house was rather old fashioned and not very clean, but there were financial advantages living there and my wife preferred it. Furthermore, my two younger children were able to attend a French school which was very close to our house. My elder daughter went to the International School adjacent to the flats.

An indoor exercise was held once or twice a year at Versailles, under the direction and supervision of none other than the Deputy Supreme Commander, Field Marshal Lord Montgomery, known as 'Monty'. Selected officers of the rank of Colonel and above, from the five nations concerned, were detailed to attend. The usual number of officers present was about fifty. A table was set in the centre of the main hall and the officers were on either side. The various units in the exercise were represented by counters of different colours and shapes and these were moved in accordance with an approved plan, by plotters around the table.

Situations were created where different aspects of the operation became apparent and then the plotting would stop, and an officer called out by name to assess the situation facing one side or the other, to explain what action should be taken to redeem the fortunes of the side he was representing.

To my surprise, my name was called and I was expected to speak. The situation was, that the enemy forces were advancing on a port, which had communication with the mainland, and it seemed they would either attack the port with a view to opening up communications with the sea, or as a springboard to attacks on the mainland.

I began by saying that the obvious action to be taken by the defending forces would be to contain the enemy's advance as best we could with the fighter bombers and light tactical bombers at our immediate disposal, but these would not be enough to hold out indefinitely and reinforcements would be required from the sea and from Bomber Command and the USAF bomber Groups.

The operations were in No. 83 Group area and the advance of the enemy had been reported by reconnaissance planes using 83 Group bases. It was therefore up to the AOC of No. 83 Group to report to the C.-in-C. of 2nd Tactical Air Force. The C.-in-C. 2nd TAF would call his staff together to discuss the situation and recommend to the C.-in-C. of AFCE that all available fighter bombers should keep pressure on the attacking forces and that the Supreme Commander should request bombers from Bomber Command and artillery support from the Royal Navy. A signal to this effect would be sent to SHAPE and again SHAPE would hold a meeting of staff officers and take action to request Bomber Command the USAF and the Royal Navy for support.

I went on to say that all this would take time which was so important in mobile warfare and that the news of the enemy attack would be reported in the newspapers in London before the Supreme Commander got to hear about it! I also said that one easy way of improving communications would be to eliminate AAFCE because it was serving no useful purpose. While I was expounding these views, I heard a lot of whispers and giggles and I feared that I may have said something quite ridiculous, but I did not feel penitent and when I finished, to my surprise, I got applause, which was unusual at such a meeting. When the meeting was over and I was putting my papers together, two ADCs from the Field Marshal's table came to me with a message from 'Monty', to the effect that he was very impressed by what I had to say and congratulated me on my speech, I asked them to convey to the Field Marshal my appreciation for his message.

One day when I was attending the Air Display at Le Bourget, I met Bill Ballantyne whom I had known well in Lima. Then he was the De Havilland representative for the whole of South America and visited Lima quite frequently. He told me that he was now the Aerospace Manager for Armstrong Siddeley Engines Ltd., and had a vacancy on his staff for an assistant Sales Manager and would like to know if I was interested. Indeed I was, and the account he gave me of the living conditions and the duties that would be required suited me very well. I would first have to inform my C.-in-C. of my intentions and then go to an interview in Coventry with the directors of Armstrong Siddeley Engines Ltd.

I think Basil Embry was genuinely disappointed when I told him what I had in mind. He said that he was prepared to recommend me for promotion in my next appointment and to nominate me for the IDC. I explained that the recommendation for the IDC would be compromised by the knowledge that I had been given the same opportunity by Sir Sholto Douglas and for reasons which I had already known, I would not be a welcome candidate eight years after my first opportunity. I knew Sir Basil very well and we had two or three long conversations together, comparing notes on our respective future plans. In particular he was anxious about my finances because he knew that I had three children destined for boarding-school. I told him that with my new salary and my pension I should be able to continue as at present. My pension would be reduced because I was under age for the maximum qualification.

I then went up to Coventry and had a pleasant interview with the Managing Director and the General Manager of Armstrong Siddeley.

They told me that they were satisfied and would be pleased if I would work for the company and they would confirm this. I went back to Fontainbleau and wrote my letter of resignation to the C.-in-C. My retirement would take effect from 31.7.55. My service in the RAF was ending after 27 years and I had enjoyed every moment of it. I had been privileged to meet many interesting and important people and to travel and work in foreign countries. All my postings had been to my liking and what's more, in my future employment, I would keep in touch with my friends from the RAF and hopefully, I would be able to entertain them occasionally on my expense account! Following a two year period based in Coventry, I was moved to Bristol as Aero Sales Manager for Bristol Siddeley Engines Ltd. Subsequently, on the take-over of Bristol Siddeley Engines Ltd., by Rolls-Royce Engines Ltd., I decided the time had come for me to leave industry, particularly as I had recently become Trustee to a large estate, which had belonged to my aunts, and would necessitate frequent visits to Scotland in order to wind up the affairs.

So it was in 1961 I gave up my job and with my family settled down in the country near Chipping Sodbury, Gloucestershire. Sadly, in 1978, my wife Jane died after a long illness, and in due course I married Elizabeth, the widow of Dr Eric Griffiths, who at the time of his sudden death in 1977, was Medical Officer to Rolls-Royce Engines Ltd., at Filton. We now live happily together and our children, stepchildren and grandchildren are frequent visitors to our home.